Performing Twentieth-Century Music

Performing Twentieth-Century Music

A Handbook for Conductors and Instrumentalists

Arthur Weisberg

Yale University Press   New Haven and London

Designed by Sonia L. Scanlon

Set in Torino type by The Composing Room of Michigan, Inc., Grand Rapids, Michigan.

Printed in the United States of America by Vail Ballou, Binghamton, New York.

Library of Congress Cataloging-in-Publication Data

Weisberg, Arthur.

    Performing twentieth-century music: a handbook for conductors and instrumentalists / Arthur Weisberg.

      p.   cm.

    Includes index.

    ISBN 0-300-05010-0

    1. Music—Interpretation (Phrasing, dynamics, etc.) 2. Music—20th century—Performance. 3. Conducting. 4. Musical meter and rhythm. I. Title.

    MT75.W38 1993

    781.4'3—dc20   93-4003

               CIP

               MN

10 9 8 7 6 5 4 3 2 1

ents

Introduction

The twentieth century has been a remarkable period in the evolution of musical composition, an era of unprecedented exploration and experimentation. The changes have often baffled both the listener and the performer. Inevitably, many of the experiments have led to dead-ends, but others have opened roads to promising new musical territory. The results of many of these explorations have been taken into the body of continuing knowledge. Artists, like scientists, are always seeking new principles, which will be little understood at first. The problem for musicians, and it is a difficult one, is to discover which are the true and lasting principles, and which pass with the moment. It is not a performer's job, however, to predict, but to perform as well as possible. To do this, performers must understand the composer's intention. We must do our best to present their ideas and not worry about historical judgments. The purpose of this book is to help instrumentalists and conductors follow the diverse paths taken by composers in the twentieth century.

Many of the problems in performing twentieth-century music are related to rhythm. This book, intended for the seasoned performer as well as the novice, sets out specific methods and exercises for mastering such rhythmic complexities as irregular meters and cross-rhythms. If instrumentalists need a practical understanding of these concepts to perform the music properly, conductors need to augment their technique to lead an ensemble through complicated rhythms. Two chapters on conducting explain and show natural arm motions and conducting patterns that can accurately convey these rhythms. These exercises can be learned and practiced by individual performers or can be adapted for classroom teaching. Once assimilated, they should make for better performances of twentieth-century music and add to its enjoyment by musicians and audiences alike.

Chapter 1
Elements of Twentieth-Century Rhythm

Rhythm is a regular recurrence of strong and weak beats. The key word is *regular.* Regularly recurring beats, whether in groups of two, three, four, six, or eight, have been the foundation of all Western music for the past few hundred years.

Only rarely have irregular meters been used, most notably 5/4 in Rimsky-Korsakov's *Russian Easter Overture,* Tchaikovsky's Sixth Symphony, and Ravel's *Daphnis and Chloë.* Igor Stravinsky, however, changed all that. Stravinsky was one of the first composers to make irregular meters an integral part of his music. In it we find such meters as 5/8, 7/16, and 11/4. His music continues to create severe problems for most musicians because they have had practically no training in dealing with the irregular meters. The foremost problem is one of counting, and since these groupings deal mostly with fives and sevens it is essential that musicians learn how to handle them. But before discussing the reasons why they are difficult it would be best to review how one counts the more normal meters and groupings.

Music students spend much of their time practicing the regular groupings of two, three, and four. During this stage the student will actually count the number of units on each beat, such as four sixteenth notes on each quarter note. In practicing this grouping over and over the student eventually reaches the point of being able to play four notes on a beat without actually counting the individual notes. In other words, the student has assimilated four on a beat. Assimilation of this kind is essential because although counting is nothing more than a mechanical process, it can easily get in the way of the music. A good analogy is reading words: having to see each letter individually before comprehending the word makes for a very slow reader. Anything that would slow down a musician would show up in the music as a technical deficiency.

The same assimilation takes place with threes, except that this group is a little easier because it contains fewer notes. It has been shown that the larger the grouping, the harder it is to assimilate as a single entity. This is one of the reasons that fives and sevens are more difficult than threes and fours.

Experienced musicians have little trouble with sixes and eights because such groupings are almost always broken down into smaller ones. Six, for example, presents us with three choices: three groups of two, two groups of three, and one group of six:

Too often (and this is also true of older music) the composer will simply write a "6" over the group of notes:

This leaves it to the performer to decide which way to subdivide the group. Subdividing inevitably introduces accents (part of its purpose), which may not be what the composer intended. It is much better for the composer to avoid ambiguity by choosing the proper notation from one of the figures shown in the first example. In any case, when we do subdivide six, we do it in a symmetrical way, either by twos or by threes.

Neither five nor seven can be subdivided into symmetrical units—hence the difficulty in performing such groupings of notes. The 5/8 meter, for example, can be subdivided in the following ways:

The first two examples are by far the most common, although the third, five eighth notes with no subdivisions, is not unusual. The solution to the performance of a difficult rhythm depends completely on its tempo; what is hard to count when fast may be easy to count when slow, and vice versa. The first two examples of 5/8 usually occur at a fast tempo. The performer then subdivides each measure into either two eighth notes (equal to a quarter note) and three eighth notes (equal to a dotted quarter) or three and two. This situation, the juxtaposition of two and three, is the most basic rhythmic statement in the twentieth century.

Why is this rhythm so difficult to play? After all, it is simple to describe mathematically: the dotted quarter is one-third slower than the quarter—that is, 33.3 percent slower, a ratio of 3:2. Mathematical descriptions, however, are not musical (metrical) ones, so they are of no help to the performer. What the musician needs is a practical way of counting rhythms.

The following metrical units are the foundation on which all traditionally notated rhythms are built:

Their relation to one another is easily perceived: each value is half as long as the preceding one. This halving or doubling is similar to that of the octave, which is related in frequency by the ratio 2:1. But this "instinctual" recognition only occurs where exact multiples are concerned. The musician's training does not involve percentages, but it is common to speak of playing twice as fast or twice as slow.

When we have to play a quarter note followed by a dotted quarter we know we cannot relate them by percentages. But they are related by the unit common to them both: the eighth note. Of course there are other, smaller common units such as sixteenth, thirty-second, and sixty-fourth notes, but these would go by much too quickly to be of any use in counting. This situation demonstrates a basic rule about playing the irregular meters: it is *always* necessary to keep the speed of the common unit (in the case of 5/8, the eighth note) in mind when performing these meters.

Counting

Counting is something that musicians can never get away from completely. It refers to keeping track of the steady flow of beats in a measure, whether subdivided or not. Though different musicians have different ways of counting, the less one's attention has to be given to that task the better. Spending a lot of mental energy on counting means that less is available for the other aspects of performance. One of the most common ways of counting is also one of the worst, that is, tapping the foot. We see it so often that I am sure students think it is the right way to count. Not only is it distracting to other musicians and the audience, particularly if it is audible, but it means that the player is following the tapping instead of listening to the other musicians or watching the conductor. And it is all too easy for the foot to follow the difficulties of the music and slow down as they appear. If one goes to a chamber music concert and notices that several of the players are tapping but one player's tapping does not synchronize with that of the others, what does this say about the music making? Even if tapping could be condoned, in a complex meter like 5/8 the inner units, the eighth notes, are often simply too fast to tap.

Musicians must develop an *inner* way of counting, one that wastes as little energy as possible. The counting must be silent and internal. In reading, if a person mouths the words then the reading will go very slowly. Most people learn to internalize the process so that the words seem to flow with little friction and are understood effortlessly. Counting in music can be done in a similar way.

It is difficult to say why counting is easy for some musicians and hard for others. An inherent talent can explain some of the difference, but a good portion has to do with one's conception of counting. Some musicians seem to be afraid of letting go of the counting process, which they see as a lifeline. One can tell by looking at the players' individual parts whether they count easily or not. Some parts are so full of pencil markings that it is hard to see the notes. These players obviously do not trust themselves to keep the beat in their heads.

Being at ease has to do partly with what we might call pattern recognition. Up until the twentieth century, rhythms fell into a relatively small number of patterns. Here are a few of the most common:

These patterns can be learned so that one does not have to count them. But they become internalized only through constant practice, after which recognizing and distinguishing them from one another takes no conscious thought.

Let's look more closely at one of these patterns:

The obvious problem in learning this pattern is dealing with the sixteenth. There are two approaches. The first counts the sixteenths from the beginning; after counting three, we arrive at the place for the fourth. This certainly works, but it is cumbersome and blocks the flow of the rhythm. The other approach attaches the sixteenth to the *next* beat (the next dotted eighth) so that it is played as an upbeat to that beat. These are radically different views of the same rhythm.

Let's look at a similar problem:

Should one count all the way through the measure to know when to play the sixteenth, or should one just wait for the next measure to come around and play a sixteenth upbeat to it?

Here is another familiar rhythmic pattern:

The same two approaches can be applied. We can count the rhythm from the beginning of the measure and from the beginning of each successive beat, or we can consider the sixteenth note, together with the following eighth, to be an upbeat to the next dotted eighth. This rhythm, incidentally, is the most awkward of all traditional rhythms. My conducting teacher, Jean Morel, a percussionist as well as a pianist who had an excellent sense of rhythm, refused to conduct Beethoven's Seventh Symphony because its first movement is built entirely on this fast siciliano-like rhythm. He was convinced that most musicians could not play the rhythm correctly. In most performances one hears, it comes out as a cross between the written rhythm and the following two rhythms:

The critical note for establishing the rhythm is the third eighth note. It usually comes too soon and consequently is too long. The thing to keep in mind is that the third eighth note is an upbeat to the next note. Always imagine the rhythm as: *one* . . . three-*one* . . . three-*one*, etc. When this is firmly in mind, the sixteenth can be added as part of the eighth upbeat, taking care not to disturb the placement of the eighth.

It is only possible to place a beat as an upbeat to the next rhythmic point if one knows when the next note is coming. If not, one is forced to count inner units to make sure of arriving with the next beat. Try to visualize the passage from one beat to the next as an arc, that is, a curved line traveling from one beat to the next:

The moment the curve starts, it predicts where it will land. We do not have to wait for it to complete its path, since the curve's end will mirror its beginning. This idea is particularly pertinent to conducting, but also has great importance for all performers. If one knows where the next beat will fall, many rhythms become much easier to realize. The alternative is to start from square one, construct the rhythm, and find out only as the next beat is occurring whether the construction was right. Of course, by that time it is too late to make any adjustments, something that could have been done if one had sensed when the next beat was *going to* arrive.

This brings us back to the idea of assimilating groups of notes. One must always be aware of the units in a group going by, but they should be sensed as silent pulses rather than counted as numbers. Most musicians will be able to do this for the standard groupings—two, three, four, six, and eight—but most likely will not have tackled fives or sevens.

The 5/8 example only involves counting twos and threes, the most basic groups that all musicians are expected to have assimilated. Combinations of twos and threes occur in all irregular meters, but when the music is fast having to change rapidly from one to the other is what causes the difficulty. This is because it is not possible to set up a regular beat, and without constant awareness of the inner units the player will quickly fall out of step.

The relationship of two to three, although crucial to twentieth-century music, is far from new. It was fairly common in baroque music and was called a *hemiola:*

In this example the hemiola is in the second and third measures. In triple meter, where hemiolas occur, the normal movement of the slower note values involves either quarter notes or dotted half notes. The hemiola was a way of introducing a different speed of note, the half note, which ordinarily did not appear as a regularly occurring unit in triple meter. The hemiola was used almost exclusively at cadences, perhaps to give the feeling of a ritardando. Composers at this point in musical history would never have thought of changing the meter to 2/4 for three measures:

Even as late as the end of the nineteenth century most composers were unwilling to change meters except at the start of large sections of a work. Brahms, for example, used the hemiola extensively. It enabled him to apparently change the meter from two to three, or vice versa, as often as he wished without having to change the time signature. In much of Brahms's music the meter is purposely ambiguous—a compositional device that contributes to his music's distinctive flavor. The counting of these hemiolas is fairly simple because they usually occur at slower tempos.

The following example, from Aaron Copland's *El Salon Mexico,* shows a typical twentieth-century use of twos and threes:

The measures alternate between 6/8 and 3/4, with the inner unit, the eighth, remaining at the same speed. This is often indicated by the following notational device:

This is stated as "eighth equals eighth."

Groupings of two and three can appear in meters other than five or seven. The following groupings are quite common: 8/8 = 3+3+2, 3+2+3, or 2+3+3. These groupings properly fall into the 8/8 meter rather than 4/4 because 4/4 implies a measure with four quarter notes, whereas 8/8 allows a wider range of possibilities.

In 9/8 there is no analogue to 4/4 = 8/8, which means that 9/8 can appear either in its traditional form of 3+3+3 or as any combination of 2+2+2+3. Similarly 10/8 and 11/8 can contain many different combinations of twos and threes:

In the following example from Stravinsky's *L'Histoire du soldat* the meter changes almost from measure to measure:

Even though this piece was written more than seventy years ago, it is still very tricky to perform. Twentieth-century music contains countless examples of changing meter, so any conscientious musician must master the techniques necessary for their performance.

Thus far we have been discussing ways to subdivide the irregular meters. But it is just as common to have to play the fives or sevens without subdividing, in other words, to play all of the inner notes with no discernible accents, just as one would play a group of four sixteenths on a quarter without accenting any of them. A quintuplet in this context would mean five *independent* notes, not 2+3, and certainly not two sixteenths followed by a triplet of sixteenths:

Musicians practice the normal groupings (two, three, and four) thousands of times more than the irregular groupings. This is one of the main reasons that fives and sevens give them trouble.

Exercises for the Irregular Meters

To learn to play groups of five and seven evenly and with no accents, the following exercises are essential. Set a metronome to 40. The first exercise is just for quintuplets:

The purpose of the exercise is to learn to experience the group of five as a single entity. For a while you will have to count the individual notes to be sure that you tap exactly five: at this point, tapping rather than playing is all that is needed. The difficulty is to have the right speed of note immediately. Once you have attained the right speed, it is easy to maintain it. A similar exercise will help with septuplets:

Once these two exercises have been mastered, move on to the next level of difficulty:

This is the central exercise that should become part of your practice routine to develop and maintain proficiency with fives and sevens.

Earlier I mentioned that it might not be possible to assimilate a septuplet without subdividing it. Certainly it is beyond the capacity of many musicians. Therefore it may be necessary divide the seven into a four plus a three. Special care should be taken, however, to avoid accenting the first beat of the three.

In a class setting, this exercise should also be done by groups of students, so that each student plays only one note of the grouping:

Not only does this exercise give students more practice in counting fives (or sevens); it also helps build good ensemble by requiring students to listen to each other. The exercise is quite practical, too: there are many instances in music where a player will only have to play one or two out of a group of quintuplet sixteenths, for example, while another player might have to play other notes in that grouping:

As important as it is to be able to play fives and sevens, it is just as important to be able to pick them out when others play them. This is essential not only for accurate performance of the next example but also in order to be proficient in the rhythmic device called metric modulation, which will be taken up in chapter 3. The next example is from the Octet for Winds, by Stravinsky:

The septuplets are at a speed of sixteenth = 441. No one can count that fast, so the ability to recognize the whole grouping is essential for the conductor and the players.

The Octet for Winds is almost always conducted, but in this example the conductor's beat cannot be accurate enough to show a player only one of the seven notes unless the player can also recognize that point. The first trombonist does not have to count, for he will automatically play the right number of notes. This is no guarantee, however, that he will play them at the right speed, and if the conductor or the other players have trouble counting the fourteen notes, then they are not likely to come in correctly at the next entrance.

The following exercises, which are all done with the metronome, are designed to teach you how to hear fast groupings. The groupings range from two on a beat to seven on a beat. The exercises are only for fast notes, which the player must perceive without having to count. The top speed of a standard metronome, 208, may seem like a very fast tempo—and it is, for quarter notes. But we need the beats to be at the speed of the sixteenths, and this can range up to 400 or 500. Fortunately there are several newer metronomes that can produce these tempos, and every musician should have one of these. There is a qualitative difference between doing these exercises at a slow rather than a fast tempo. For the assimilation of large irregular groupings, mm = 208 is so slow that one cannot avoid counting the notes individually. In the beginning you may want to choose an intermediate tempo, such as mm = 300, then work up to full speed.

In the following exercises, tap once at the beginning of each group. In the exercise for recognizing quintuplets, for instance, tap once every five clicks of the metronome:

Practice the following groupings: 2+3, 3+4, 5, 2+3+2, 3+3+2, and 7. Consider the meters to be in eighths, so that the first one, 2+3, would be played:

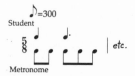

In other words, while the metronome is clicking, tap a quarter followed by a dotted quarter and continue to do this. Incidentally, this first one, in 5/8, is the most difficult because the changes from two to three occur very quickly.

At places in Stravinsky's Octet the groupings change every two beats, from sevens to fives to sixes. The problem of changing groupings from beat to beat is far from new, and even in its simplest forms—changing from two to three and from three to four—has given many musicians trouble:

The following exercise directly addresses this problem, but the exact ordering of the groupings should be changed from one practice period to the next:

In a class setting, students should alternate lines, so that the first student plays the first line twice, the second plays the second line twice, and so on. Make sure that there is one quarter rest between each line and no more. Notice that in this exercise the even groupings can also give trouble.

All of the exercises in this book, though they can and should be practiced at home by individual students, are really intended for class use. So the teacher must have an excellent rhythmic sense in order to be able to correct the students.

Cross-Rhythms

The expansion and development of rhythm in the twentieth century has taken several directions, one of which is the use of cross-rhythms. A cross-rhythm is a rhythm in one meter (time signature) played at the same time as a rhythm in another meter within the same bar lines. Each rhythm may be given its own time signature, or brackets may be used to designate one rhythm in place of an additional time signature:

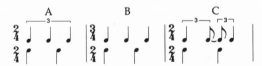

Example A illustrates the simplest cross-rhythm, 3×2, or three against two. The three notes of the triplet (bracketed) are played against the two "normal" (unbracketed) quarter notes. Though the term is recent, cross-rhythms have been used throughout musical history by most of the great composers. Usually, however, they served to create a rubato and did not demand rhythmic precision. They were also typically used in the faster tempos, where even if played precisely they would have been difficult to recognize. Contrary to most musical problems, a cross-rhythm becomes more difficult to execute the slower it is played.

Most musicians can give a fair rendering of the simplest cross-rhythms, 3×2 and 2×3, even without training in them. Let us now look at a difficult one, 4×5:

At this slow tempo few musicians could even come close to an accurate rendering. Except for the downbeat, the other three notes of the four group fall in invisible places in the 5/4 measure. We call them invisible if one cannot figure out *exactly* where they fall. Yet it should be obvious that they must fall in precise metrical places. Our problem is to find those places.

How many rhythmic points can we imagine as existing in a 4/4 measure? If we were to set a limitation on the smallest value as, say, a normal sixteenth note, the answer would be that there were sixteen points in the measure. To answer the question, then, it is necessary to set certain other limitations so that the answer is not an infinite number. These limitations concern the smallest note values to be used, and we will limit ourselves to sixty-fourths. We must also include the most common bracketed units: triplets, quintuplets, and septuplets, all down to sixty-fourths. The answer is surprisingly large: 288. In other words, a composer can choose to place a note on any of 288 rhythmic points in the 4/4 measure.

To see how the figure of 288 is arrived at, let us first review the various groupings: normal notes, here represented by four sixteenths:

triplets of sixteenths:

quintuplets of sixteenths:

septuplets of sixteenths:

These each equal the value of a quarter. Let us see if there are any coincident points among them. They all coincide at the beginning of the beat, so this would be considered *one* rhythmic point. There is only one other coincident point, which occurs where the second eighth note would fall; in other words, the third normal sixteenth coincides with the fourth triplet sixteenth:

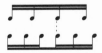

If we now add up the number of separate points we get a total of eighteen. Since our smallest unit is the sixty-fourth and there are four of them on a sixteenth, the same procedure reveals that there are eighteen points within each sixteenth. And since there are sixteen sixteenths in a 4/4 measure, we multiply sixteen by eighteen and get 288.

This is a roundabout way of saying that a composer can conceive of a rhythm that can fall on any of the 288 points or on some combination of them. The musician's task is to be able to locate and understand any of those points. The method for accomplishing this task will now be explained.

The Least Common Denominator and the Rhythmic Grid

Before we begin, a few words about mathematics are in order. Only basic arithmetic is required for solving any of the problems in this book. Algebra could also be used, but algebra is concerned more with the pure manipulation of numbers and ratios than with specific musical quantities. For that reason, and because many musicians are uncomfortable with algebra, we will only use multiplication and division, and these will always deal specifically with the metric units being discussed at the moment.

Let us imagine that a player is having trouble playing the following example:

The triplet of quarters in the 2/4 measure makes this a cross-rhythm of 3×2. If a player does not understand the inner workings of this measure, even though it is the simplest possible example, then the placement of the second and third triplets will have to be guessed. In order to eliminate any guesswork, the following rules can be applied to this and any other difficult cross-rhythm, such as 3×5, or 4×7. Incidentally, this cross-rhythm would be solved in the same manner if written as two separate meters:

In all problems of this kind the first task is to relate the two metric families (the normal and triplet families) by finding a single metric unit that can fit both of them. In other words, we must find a common denominator, also called the least common denominator (LCD). The LCD is the smallest number into which both of the numbers in question can be divided, in this case the *two* quarters and the *three* triplet quarters. You find the least common denominator of two numbers by multiplying them: two times three equals six. Six then is the least common denominator.

Step 1: Find the LCD.
Step 2: Make a rhythmic grid. In the 2/4 example, the grid will have six strokes since six is the LCD.

Each of the two quarter notes contains three of the strokes.

Step 3: Determine the metrical value of the strokes.

The three strokes in the quarter must equal triplet eighths:

This is now the completed rhythmic grid for this problem. It is composed of metrical units that are common to both the normal quarters and the triplet quarters. Every note in the measure will fall somewhere on the grid.

Step 4: Transfer the problem rhythm (the triplet quarters) onto the grid, using ties wherever needed.

At this point let me introduce a basic rule of musical notation, which I call the equivalency, or family, rule. The equivalency rule states that the relationships between normal notes in a family—two half notes in a whole note, two quarter notes in a half note, and so on—hold for bracketed notes as well. Thus, a triplet quarter contains two triplet eighths or four triplet sixteenths. We can even consider dotted notes to be members of a family, so that a dotted quarter will contain four dotted sixteenths.

This rule can help us with step 4 of the method. We want to know how many of the grid units to assign to each triplet quarter. There are two ways to arrive at the answer. In one, the equivalency rule tells us that each triplet quarter contains two triplet eighths. We would therefore tie together each two eighths. The other way to arrive at this result is to divide the six grid units by three, the number of notes in the problem rhythm, and find that each of these notes gets two of the grid units. Although the problem rhythm can be easily played by looking at example 39, there is still one more step.

Step 5: Rewrite the problem rhythm into its simplest form, using ties only when necessary.

We shall see that with complicated rhythms, ties can be very confusing. The final answer to the sample problem should look like this:

Chapter 2
Rewriting and Composite Rhythms

Step 5 of the method for solving cross-rhythms included the word *rewrite*. What we are doing is rewriting a difficult rhythm so that we can see and understand exactly where every note in it falls in the measure. The rewriting does not alter the way the rhythm sounds; it simply makes it much easier to play.

In addition to the five steps for rewriting cross-rhythms, there are two general rules to keep in mind. *The time signature of the original measure must not be changed.* For instance, it would be possible to give an equivalent rendering of the last example (p. 20) by changing the meter to 6/8:

This is not a good practice, however. All players should have the same time signature unless a composer intentionally assigns them different signatures. *Use beams wherever possible, rather than stems and flags.* Isolated stems come from vocal writing and are intended to show word or syllable changes. This is always confusing to read because it is hard to tell where the beats fall. Often in such notation musicians have been forced to put strokes into the music to help define the beat placement:

The main purpose in rewriting is to make the rhythm as simple to understand as possible. One way to do this is to make the main beats of the measure visible. Beams delineate the beats naturally:

Although the cross-rhythm is only one of the types of rhythm needing to be rewritten, at the moment we will continue with it because the method for solving it can be applied to all rewriting problems.

Let us look at another fairly common cross-rhythm, 3×4:

If one cannot play it correctly, then it needs to be rewritten. Musicians who do not know how to rewrite would be forced to fake their way through it. Educated faking does have a place in performance, but not where accuracy is concerned. As for all difficult rhythms, the slower the tempo, the more difficult it would be to fake, and one can be quite far off by the end of the measure.

Step 1: Find the LCD. $3 \times 4 = 12$.

Step 2: Make a rhythmic grid. Place twelve strokes in the 4/4 measure.

Step 3: Determine the metric value of the strokes. Three per quarter note = triplet eighths.

Step 4: Transfer the problem rhythm onto the grid by using ties:

Step 5: Rewrite the rhythm in its simplest form, doing away with unnecessary ties:

Obviously, eliminating the first three tied triplet eighth notes and replacing them with a quarter in no way changes the way that the note sounds, and proper notation would never allow so many notes to be tied together.

The Explanatory Bracket

Explanatory brackets are a twentieth-century notational development. Let us look at an example that will show why they have become necessary:

= ?

If we ask musicians to give the equivalent value in normal rhythmic units for this example, we would get at least two different results: quarter note or half note. The reasoning behind each answer is that, on the one hand, seven is so close to eight that we should go in that direction (larger) and have the seven sixteenths be equal to eight sixteenths, or a half note. The other answer says that we should always follow the triplet rule, whereby the three triplet notes are in the place of two normal notes—in other words, always go smaller instead of larger. In fact, composers do not agree on which is the correct method, and we find both in use. The value of the explanatory bracket is that it allows us to know which method is being used. The method calling for seven going down to four, or five going down to four, is the one that is used by most composers.

Consider these examples of quintuplets and sextuplets:

Here we see quintuplets covering three, four, and six beats, and septuplets covering 4/8, 5/8, 6/8, and 4/4. They are all quite different from each other, and yet the traditional bracket simply called them quintuplets or septuplets. Situations such as these show the need for a different kind of bracket. It is called the explanatory bracket, and it gives us all of the information that is needed. Here is another example using explanatory brackets:

What must the time signature be in this measure? Without understanding the brackets, musicians could give as many as six different answers.

We are all used to the triplet bracket, but what does it actually mean? In a 2/4 measure we find a triplet of eighth notes. The triplet bracket is so common that everyone takes it for granted that the three eighths are in the same time as two normal eighths. All brackets are as easy to understand as the triplet bracket if we read them in a similar way. Thus a quintuplet bracket of sixteenths is played in the same time as four normal sixteenths, or a normal quarter:

All brackets in this book are of the square type. The familiar curved bracket has fallen out of favor because it can be confused with the articulation marking called a slur:

The square bracket in the first example should be read as follows: five sixteenth notes in the space (or time) of four sixteenth notes, making the whole group equal to a quarter note. For this type of bracket both sets of metric units must be the same; that is, if the five of the bracket refers to sixteenth notes, then the four of the bracket must also refer to sixteenths. This type of bracket by itself never specifically tells us what the metric unit is, but that should always be obvious from a look at the notes under the bracket.

The brackets should always be read in the following manner:

This bracket says: "Five eighths in the space of three eighths." (Some musicians would say, "in the *time* of," but they mean the same thing.) Saying the sentence this way tells one precisely what the bracket is worth: three eighths. It would be incorrect to leave the last word out of the sentence because then there could be confusion as to whether the five eighths were equal to three sixteenths, eighths, or quarters.

Here are some practice examples to help understand explanatory brackets:

Read as: Five eighths in the space of four eighths.

Five quarters in the space of three quarters.

Four sixteenths in the space of five sixteenths.

Seven quarters in the space of four quarters.

Other types of explanatory brackets that one sees are more explicit and allow different metric units to be mixed:

In this book, however, I shall use only the 5:4 type of explanatory bracket because it is the one most widely used by composers.

The most frequent cross-rhythms are:

$3\times2, 2\times3$
$3\times4, 4\times3$
$3\times5, 5\times3$
$4\times5, 5\times4$

If we use quarter-note meters, then the first cross-rhythm (3×2) would be a 2/4 measure, with three notes played against it (triplet quarters). Its opposite (2×3) would be a 3/4 measure. In other words, the first number is played against the second. Here is a chart for these cross-rhythms:

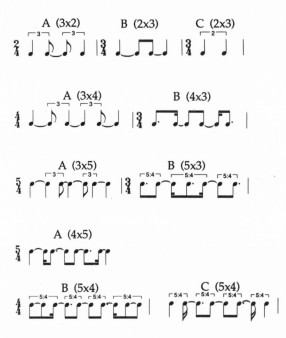

The choice of notation for the final rewriting is something that must be decided by each student. A careful look at the two 5×4 examples shows that they are equivalent, and although the first has a few more ties, some musicians might think that it is easier to read.

Notice that all these rewritten cross-rhythms are mirror images, that is, the rhythm proceeds to the middle of the measure, then reverses itself to the end of the measure. This characteristic provides a way to check whether you have chosen the right solution. Another obvious way of checking is to make sure that all the rewritten notes are of the same length.

Practice writing the following cross-rhythms:

1. 4/4, 7×4:

LCD = 28

2. 6/4, 5×6:

LCD = 30

3. 5/4, 6×5:

LCD = 30

Rewriting Other Rhythms

Let's look at a rhythmic example from Charles Ives's *Three Places in New England:*

THREE PLACES IN NEW ENGLAND, by Charles Ives. Copyright © 1935 and 1976, Mercury Music Corporation. Used by Permission of the Publisher, Theodore Presser Company.

Notice that the explanatory bracket is not in the example, for it did not yet exist when Ives wrote the piece (1903–1914). But it cannot mean anything except five quarters in the space of four quarters. Could we expect the first violin section, which carries the phrase, to play it correctly? Unfortunately, we cannot. I once gave the score of *Three Places in New England* to a celebrated conductor who planned to do the work with one of the world's leading orchestras. The conductor, who understood explanatory brackets perfectly well, chose to change the quintuplet values into triplets rather than contend with the inability of the players to render the passage correctly. Changing to a triplet version resulted in the players' being together, but in the process they changed the rhythm asked for by the composer, something that conscientious musicians should avoid if at all possible.

The rewriting procedure I have outlined for cross-rhythms would obviate the need to alter such passages as this as well. Let us follow it for the Ives example:

1. Find the LCD $5 \times 4 = 20$.
2. Make a rhythmic grid: twenty strokes in the 4/4 measure.
3. Determine the metric value of the strokes: divide twenty by the number of beats in the measure to get five units for each quarter note. Five metric units on a quarter must be quintuplet sixteenths.
4. Transfer the original rhythm onto the grid using ties.

To do the transferring easily, we must remember the equivalency rule, in which members of the same note family relate in a simple way (for example, quarter = four sixteenths). Start with the first quintuplet half note. A half note, within any family, contains eight sixteenths; therefore we tie the first eight grid units:

Then treat each of the notes of the original passage similarly:

5. Rewrite, eliminating unnecessary ties.

This rhythm, though fairly complex, is completely understandable, and once understood it could certainly be played accurately after a reasonable amount of practice.

The next example, from a work by Luigi Dallapiccola, goes a step beyond the Ives because it involves more than rewriting a cross-rhythm.

Rewriting is primarily a way of relating the disparate notes in a measure by finding what is common between them. The disparate notes are *always* those which are under a bracket, like the triplets in the Dallapiccola example. In rewriting cross-rhythms we first found a common denominator (LCD), which we used to fill the measure (the rhythmic grid); all rhythmic units fit somewhere on the grid. But that method will not work for this example: the rhythmic grid for triplet quarters and normal quarters is made up of triplet eighths:

We cannot transfer the Dallapiccola example because there is no place on the grid for the first triplet note:

Therefore we must instead find a rhythmic unit that fits (is common to) everything in this measure. A simple rule may help: *the common unit will always be found in the bracketed family.* So we know that we are looking for a triplet unit; it is only a matter of deciding what size that unit should be (sixteenths, eighths, quarters), and since all members of a family fit each other, we should look not at the triplets but at the smallest normal units involved. In this example it is the eighth rests that cause the problem. We therefore need the largest triplet that fits in an eighth: a triplet of sixteenths. The triplet sixteenth is the key to solving this problem and hence will comprise the grid units:

In doing the transfer we must remember the equivalency rule, which tells us that whereas a normal eighth note contains three of the triplet grid units, the triplet quarter contains four.

Here is how the rhythm looks after the final rewriting:

One of the rules for rewriting is that the rewritten rhythm should be in its simplest form. Ultimately the choice of form is up to the individual, and people do come up with different answers. We can see this clearly in the present example. There are at least four ways to "spell" the second beat of the measure:

The chosen form should be the easiest one to read, but the choice should also involve how the measure will be counted. The first two are better counted in eighths, while the last two lend themselves to counting in quarters.

We will now speak about a metric fact concerning bracketed notes, which although self-evident, is not something that most musicians have considered. The following example is about triplets, but would be applicable to any of the bracketed units:

The first note of each group is a triplet quarter. Although each group lasts a different amount of time, the first triplet quarter has exactly the same value (length) regardless of group. The significance of this will become evident in some later discussions.

Here is another example to rewrite:

The approach to this problem should be the same as for the last; that is, the grid unit that we are looking for must first of all be a triplet. The size of the triplet depends on the smallest normal value in the measure: a sixteenth. The largest triplet that fits in a sixteenth is made up of thirty-seconds; this will be the grid unit. How many groups of triplets are in this 3/8 measure? If you know how many normal sixteenths there are (six), then you also know that there are six groups of thirty-second triplets:

Following our method we get the answer:

In the past, triplets that start on the offbeat were extremely rare, but today we find them in the works of many composers, such as Stefan Wolpe, Luigi Dallapiccola, and Ralph Shapey. Here is a chart made up of triplets that shows the relationships that exist in this family. The smallest unit is a thirty-second (one could, of course, make a chart down to sixty-fourths). The chart can be considered as a grid in a 4/4 measure. Any size of triplet will find a place on the grid. In other words, the triplet can start at any point in the measure, and by using the equivalency rule one can rewrite it fairly easily:

Most musicians looking at the following example for the first time would say that it is incorrectly written:

There appears to be too much time in the first measure and not enough in the second, although the total of the two measures adds up correctly to four quarters. On realizing this, many would say that the bar line is in the wrong place. But where should it be put? A similar question is, Where is the middle of the triplet? It appears to be on the second note. Visually that is correct, but the visual exists in space, whereas music exists in time. A note exists not as a point but as a line continuing until its allotted time is used up:

The second triplet quarter in the example is of a length that causes it to run over into the next measure. This becomes clear when we rewrite the example using the triplet eighth as the LCD:

This type of notation was used even in the classical era:

Although visual and musical space are different, the placement of notes on the page can either help or hinder the performer. Ideally, the spacing of rhythms should conform to the amount of time that they take. This unconsciously helps the eye understand them. There are unfortunately too many examples like the following that obscure rather than aid:

All bracketed rhythms should be spaced properly to help promote their correct rendering even by musicians who lack knowledge of their inner workings.

A final complexity with triplets involves a triplet within a triplet. This example, written in 1913, is from the clarinet part to Arnold Schoenberg's *Pierrot Lunaire:*

The conductor is beating in four, and the clarinetist would want to know where the second quarter falls in relation to the passage. The problem could be avoided if the clarinetist were to count in half notes, but these are really too slow to work. A simple bit of rewriting brings us closer to an answer, but not close enough:

This has not taken into account the triplet within a triplet. To do this we must find a further common unit (a triplet) to fit all parts of the first two quarters of the measure. Neither of the following choices works, because they relate primarily to the normal eighth or sixteenth and hence do not fit the triplet within the triplet:

The LCD is eighteen, or $2 \times 3 \times 3$—the two normal quarters times the three triplet quarters times the three notes of the inner triplet. We now see that everything fits somewhere:

This whole process would be necessary *only if* there were a desire to be completely accurate. Again, the choice is part of the interpretive process. An intelligent choice would depend on the musician knowing the style of the work. At this point in Schoenberg's development his style was highly romantic, so the musical phrase could be interpreted more freely. This passage is an excellent example of the difference between accuracy and flow. One can, by working quite hard, achieve accuracy, but at the cost of flow. A compromise can be reached by being accurate with the placement of the first inner triplet note and then intuiting the rest (educated faking).

  This next example is the same type of problem as the offbeat triplet and can be solved in the same manner:

Find the quintuplet value that fits within the smallest normal value, and make a grid of those units (the ties have already been inserted):

The equivalency rule says that the normal eighth gets five units whereas the quintuplet eighth gets four. The final version is:

Admittedly this is a difficult rhythm to play, but at least we can see exactly where the notes should fall.

Educated Faking

Sometimes knowing where the notes fall is not enough to be able to play them. Consider the quintuplet thirty-seconds in the last example: with a quarter speed of 50, the quintuplets are at a speed of eighth note = $100 \times 5 = 500$. Musicians can certainly play that fast, but no one can count the individual notes. In other words, the method chosen to perform a difficult rhythmic problem depends on its speed. If the present example were at a speed of eighth note = 40, then the quintuplets would be at a speed of 200 and could be counted, although still with some difficulty. There are two other ways of playing this example, and both call for educated faking.

Faking, in this context, applies only to rhythm; it is *educated* faking because the rhythm is completely understood intellectually, though the inner units are too fast to count. The rhythms under discussion are all fives or sevens. We can take some comfort from recognizing that not only does the performer find the units too fast to count, but the listener and even the composer do too. This is not to condone inaccuracy, but one must realize that there are limits to human perception.

The rhythm that we saw in the last example, although too fast to count, can still be realized with a high degree of accuracy. We can see that the second quintuplet note in that example occurs immediately before the second normal quarter in the measure. If one then plays only the first two quintuplets, as in the next example, those two notes will in effect set up a speed of their own.

The player, while placing those notes as accurately as possible, can also be aware of the new speed of note that has been created. Keeping this new speed of note in mind, the player can try to continue it, and with some practice can produce a result that is quite accurate. In order to make it even more accurate, the player might notice if the last of the quintuplet notes falls just after the normal third beat of the measure.

Another method is to treat the quintuplet rhythm spatially. Think of this measure as having three quarters notated normally while the quintuplet floats above those beats:

The placement of the quintuplet units is only indicated spatially in relation to the three quarter notes. The spacing would actually follow the spacing seen on the original grid but need not be so precise, because spatial notation allows for some deviation. The point is that the notes need only be placed in a general relation to the normal quarters and still produce acceptable results. The more one tries to place them exactly, the less flowing they will be: instead, performers should make an interpretive decision in response to their understanding of the composer's intent. Some composers would want the rhythm to be exact, and others would want more flow. A musician needs to know the various compositional styles to make an intelligent choice.

Musicians often wonder why composers do not avoid misunderstandings by providing all of the rewritten rhythms, since many of these rhythms have little chance of being performed correctly in their original versions. Unfortunately, many composers do not know how to rewrite. But in other cases the choice of notational form is a matter of aesthetics and style. Composers who are more interested in rhythmic accuracy than in other musical parameters will favor rewritten rhythms. The aesthetic approach, by contrast, would favor the present example in its original version, which has an elegant and flowing look to it. The problem is that many musicians will not know how to play it. On the other hand, most performers, looking at the rewritten example alone, might not realize that the five quantities should produce five even notes. "Enlightened" composers may give both versions—the first to show the style and the second (usually placed as a cue above the first) to show how to play the measure.

Let's see how our new understanding of complex rhythms can help in performing such passages in a work written before the invention of explanatory brackets. The example is from Igor Stravinsky's *Petrouschka:*

The explanatory bracket is missing because it had not yet been invented, but the phrase should read 7:6. In the original version, the meter of the measure was called 7/8, but the problem is the same. Before discussing rewriting, we should know what Stravinsky had in mind. *Petrouschka* is a ballet, and the scene where this passage occurs depicts a large carnival with many different things going on at the same time. Charles Ives was also very fond of portraying several different musics happening at once, but he would often write them in different meters or even with different metronome indications. Stravinsky did not want this passage to fit with the rest of the music being played at the same time, which was a harmonic progression moving steadily on the quarters.

How can we rewrite this passage? Normally we would expect to find the LCD by multiplying 6×7. What we are really interested in, however, is how the septuplet notes fit against the three normal quarters of the measure, since normal quarters are the only other rhythmic unit that is being used. If the normal music had included all six eighths, then we would also be concerned as to how the septuplets fit against them, and we would have to go to forty-two subdivisions. Forty-two subdivisions in a 3/4 measure is difficult to imagine, let alone work with: it would require fourteen septuplets per quarter. For the purposes of this exercise, we only need twenty-one subdivisions for the grid, or seven per quarter.But when we try to transfer the septuplet eighth passage onto the grid, we seem to run into a problem. The equivalency rule says that there are two septuplet sixteenths in a septuplet eighth. When we apply this, we find that there is an entire beat of septuplets left over:

Doing the measure with forty-two subdivisions does not help—there is still a beat left over:

The answer to this dilemma has already appeared. In the previous example we see that the septuplets have been placed in the normal septuplet family of 7:4, when in reality our example belongs to another family, 7:6. Sevens and fives, as we saw earlier, can belong to several different families depending on how many normal notes they span. A quintuplet of eighth notes, for example, can be over a 3/8, 2/4, or 3/4 measure, and even if the normal units are kept at the same speed in each of the three measures, the quintuplet eighths will be different:

To find the correct number to work with, we need to divide the total of the grid units, twenty-one, by seven. This tells us that each of the septuplet eighths is equal to three of the grid units, and after all of the septuplet sixteenths are properly tied the phrase will look like this:

This rendering is much more angular and complicated-looking than the original. Again, players may not know the simple relationship that exists between the various notes in the bracketed version, something that is very evident in Stravinsky's. On the other hand, they can see exactly where the septuplets fall in comparison with the normal quarters. One could now practice the passage and be able to play it quite accurately. A word of caution, though: should you be a member of a professional orchestra and play the passage "correctly," the chances are that you will be the only one to do so, and consequently you will not be with the others. Most professional musicians and conductors would not be able to rewrite the passage, and even if they could, most would not care whether the performance of it were totally accurate. Neither, I suspect, would Stravinsky.

The last example of a rhythm that needs rewriting will seem at first to be highly complicated. But if we follow the steps we have been using, it will become almost routine. First one must understand the problem. This example is by the American composer Ralph Shapey, who regularly uses bracketed groups on various parts of the beat. The piece is his Chamber Concerto for Violin and Ensemble:

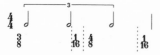

We see a 4/4 measure with a triplet of half notes that is played by two of the instruments. The other smaller measures, which add up to one 4/4 measure, are played by the rest of the group. This work requires a conductor, who will be beating the smaller measures. How do the half note triplet players know when to change notes? It is relatively rare to see 1/16 measures, but they do exist, as do measures consisting of, for example, two quarters and a triplet quarter. The biggest problem with the last is what to call it (see chapter 3).

As usual with rewriting, we need a common unit in order to make a grid. The common unit will be a triplet value fitting within the smallest normal value that is a part of the problem, which in this case is a sixteenth. The triplet that fits within a sixteenth is a thirty-second. Therefore we will have a grid of thirty-second triplets through the 4/4 measure, which will also show the little measures within it:

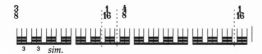

The equivalency rule tells us how many of the grid units to tie for the triplet half notes: each contains sixteen grid units. Rewriting will eliminate the unnecessary ties:

This last rewriting can definitely be played accurately, but a further refinement can be made in the first little measure. It requires us to notice that the following phrases are equivalent:

Composite Rhythm

Cross-rhythms are best learned by practicing their rewritten rhythms with a metronome, which marks the normal rhythm. If we were to listen to both rhythms together, we would hear the combination of the two, called the *composite rhythm*. One of the easiest ways to learn cross-rhythms is to know their composite rhythm.

Here are two examples of cross-rhythms and their composite rhythms:

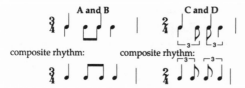

The composite rhythm would usually be written with all flags going in the same direction, but they are shown here with the flags in opposite directions to help separate the two rhythms. Knowing the composite rhythm, if we were to hear two performers playing 3×2 or 2×3, we would know immediately if they were playing correctly.

The following are the composite rhythms for the most commonly used cross-rhythms:

Of the eight examples, six are fairly easy to recognize and execute, and two (3/4—5×3, 4/4—5×4) are very hard. The difficulty abates, however, when we realize that the composite rhythms 2×3 and 3×2, for example, sound alike to a listener who is not involved with the beat. We can understand this better if we return to examples A (4×5) and B (5×4) on p. 26: in both the LCD is six, therefore one part in each has notes that are two units long, and the other part has notes that are three units long. If we adjust the tempo so that one of the six units in A and one of the six units in B are at the same speed, then the two measures will sound exactly the same:

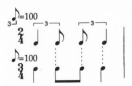

Those cross-rhythms dealing with twos, threes, and fours are rather simple because we are familiar with all of their permutations, but fives and sevens are a different matter. The example of 5×3 (p. 40) could conceivably be played as written, but would require an enormous expenditure of energy. To count the fast-moving quintuplets while at the same time emphasizing every third unit (*one*-two-three-*four*-five, one-*two*-three-four-*five*, one-two-*three*-four-five) would be beyond the capabilities of most musicians. On the other hand, the composite rhythm 3×5 is simple because it only deals with triplets, so it sounds the same to the listener as 5×3.

In the following exercise, set the metronome to play the normal quarters while you play quintuplets (5×3). To start, however, play only the first three quintuplets, which we will consider as making up a 3/4 measure. Play the first two notes so that the second metronome note falls a triplet eighth before your third quarter:

STUDENT (3 of the 5)
METRONOME (2 of the 3)

Admittedly there is a little guesswork as to when to play the second note, but this can be learned relatively quickly. The entire rhythm can then be practiced:

STUDENT
METRONOME

If one is slightly off with the second or third notes, this will be quite apparent and adjustments can easily be made. After a certain amount of practice you will suddenly become aware of the composite rhythm. The whole process, once learned, can be carried out in a very relaxed manner that produces a smooth phrase, compared with the jerky rendition that usually comes of having to count all of the fives on each beat. The other difficult cross-rhythms dealing with fives and sevens can be done this way too. In fact, using the composite rhythm is the only method that will allow conducting two meters at the same time.

The composite rhythm method has other uses as well. Consider the following example, which has three different rhythms:

In this passage, the player or the conductor would have a difficult time knowing whether all of the parts were in their proper places. But if we make a composite rhythm from the separate lines, it becomes much easier to identify any wrong placement of notes:

composite rhythm:

It is often helpful for the conductor to write the composite rhythm into the score, because only rarely will the composer have done so.

Here is another example that could benefit from the techniques of rewriting and composite rhythm:

Many musicians would consider either of the lines alone to be fairly difficult to play, let alone both at the same time. We will again skip the first step involving the LCD, as this example is not a simple cross-rhythm. Knowing automatically that we are looking for a triplet unit, we only have to decide what size it should be. First we look for the smallest normal unit that is a part of the problem—in this case, an eighth. The smallest triplet that fits on an eighth is made up of sixteenths, so the grid consists of five groups of triplet sixteenths:

For clarity, let's tie on the top for one rhythm and on the bottom for the other:

In all rewriting, one must remember that some of the tied notes may represent rests in the original. In the final version the rests must be restored:

Each line by itself is easy to play, and we only have to combine them to get the composite rhythm (arrows show the individual parts):

This rhythm is not at all difficult, and an incorrect rendering by one of the players will certainly stand out.

Chapter 3
The Metronome and Metric Modulation

Music exists in time, and therefore the ability to measure time is crucial to both composer and performer. The rhythmic structure of music, on the other hand, is directed toward describing how the individual beats relate to each other, and says nothing about how slow or fast the beats should go. Throughout much of the history of music the composer's only way of imparting this information was by such descriptive words as *adagio* (slow), *andante* (moderate), *allegro* (fast), and *presto* (very fast). Many other words were used to modify these basic terms, but they could still only give an approximate idea of the speed the composer intended. For some composers this was close enough, but many others desired greater control over the performance of their music. Several schemes had been tried. By varying the length of a string with a weight on the end of it—a pendulum—different speeds could be obtained. This proved cumbersome, and during Beethoven's lifetime Johann Maelzel, a musician and inventor, developed the clockwork metronome. Beethoven, who was very particular about the performance of his music, embraced the idea and added Maelzel metronome (mm) markings to a number of his most important compositions. Speeds on the standard metronome range from 40 beats per minute to 208. Thus, mm 60 is equivalent to one second on the clock. Metronome speeds have gradually become universally accepted, although a few composers still use the traditional descriptive words. (Some composers use both, perhaps because they feel that words add a flavor that cold-blooded numbers do not).

In twentieth-century music frequent tempo changes are the rule rather than the exception. Often the tempos are unrelated to each other, and performing the piece becomes a matter of jumping from one discrete metronome speed to another.

Deriving Metronomic Speeds

The standard set of metronome speeds is 40, 48, 56, 60, 66, 72, 76, 84, 96, 100, 108, 116, 120, 126, 132, 144, 160, and 208, although some metronomes have a few more speeds than these. The only speed among them that could be a considered universal is mm 60, or one beat per second; all of the others are arbitrary: for example, 76 is no more meaningful than 77. The manipulation of these speeds has become important to many composers, and it is therefore necessary for performers to understand how this system works.

Once the basic speed has been determined (for example, quarter = 100), it is possible to determine the speed of any other metric unit. If

♩=100   then   ♪=200   ♬=400
                             𝅗𝅥=50   o =25

These speeds are all related by a multiple of two: each is twice as fast or twice as slow as the adjacent speeds. The half note is twice as slow as the quarter, since there are two quarters in the half, so we divide 100 by two and get 50. There are four sixteenths in a quarter note, therefore it is four times as fast as the quarter, so we multiply by four to get 400. To find the speed of a sixty-fourth, we must first know how many their are in a quarter. Many musicians have forgotten the basics or have never realized that the names of the rhythmic units are given in terms of the whole note; that is, the half note divides the whole into two parts, the sixteenth divides it into sixteen parts, and so on. So the whole note contains sixty-four sixty-fourths, and the quarter note contains sixteen sixty-fourths.

The arithmetic for triplets is almost as simple as that for the normal units. Since there are three triplet eighths in a quarter, we only have to multiply 100 by three to get 300 for the speed of a triplet eighth. Similarly, a triplet sixteenth would be at a speed of 600. To determine the speed of larger triplets, the process is a bit more complicated. For example, what does a triplet quarter equal? Since the triplet quarter does not directly relate to a normal quarter by a multiple of two, we must first find a common unit from among the bracketed family—triplets in this case. From this point there are two choices for continuing, which can be called the large method and the small method. The large way asks: What normal unit does a triplet quarter fit into? The answer is a normal half note:

$$\frac{5}{8} \quad \overline{^{3}} \quad ♩ \, ♩ \, ♩ \; = \; 𝅗𝅥$$

The small way asks: What triplet unit fits into a triplet quarter? The answer is a triplet eighth:

$$\textstyle\quad \bf\musJ = \overset{3}{\musJJJ}\ ,\qquad \overset{3\rceil}{\musJ} = \overset{3\raisebox{0.3ex}{\rule{1.2em}{0.4pt}}}{\musJSJS}$$

In the first example, we see that there are three triplet quarters in a half note. Since a half note equals 50, the speed of each triplet quarter is $3 \times 50 = 150$. In the second example, we see that there are three triplet eighths in a quarter; therefore the speed of the triplet eighth is 300. The equivalency rule tells us that there are two triplet eighths in a triplet quarter; therefore we divide 300 by two and likewise get 150 as the speed of the triplet quarter. The choice of method depends on the particular problem. Sometimes the two approaches work equally well, and other times one or the other will be easier to use. When looking for the speed of a single bracketed unit, many students feel that the easiest way to solve the problem is to complete the bracket and then see what normal unit the whole group fits into:

$$\overset{3\rceil}{\musJ}\qquad \text{complete bracket with triplet quarters:}\qquad \overset{\lceil\;3\;\rceil}{\musJ\,\musJ\,\musJ}\quad \musHalf$$

By the small approach, we will look for a bracketed note that is smaller than the one in question, and for large, we will complete the bracket with the same value of note as the one in question.

Thus far we have been concerned with the speed of a single triplet quarter. This was more than just a demonstration of the arithmetic involved in calculating speed, for such things as incomplete brackets do exist in twentieth-century music, particularly where the rhythmic modulation method is used. Moreover, one needs to be able to derive single note speeds in order to solve certain other problems. If we look back at the Ives example on p. 27, which has five quarters against four quarters, we see that we have solved the problem by rewriting the fives.

Another way of solving this problem would be to find the metronomic speed of a quintuplet quarter and then count the measure in five. This problem is most easily solved by the large method, that is, by taking the quintuplet in its entirety and relating it to a normal unit. In this case, that unit is the whole note: five quarters in the space of four quarters is equivalent to a whole note. We derive the speed of a whole note from that of a quarter, mm 100, by dividing 100 by four, the number of quarters in the whole note, to get mm 25. There are five quintuplet quarters in the whole note, and each is five times as fast as the whole, so the speed of a quintuplet quarter is mm 125 (5 × 25 = 125). If the conductor or players beat this measure in five, at mm 125, it would sound exactly like the rewritten version and be much easier to play.

Which method to use depends on the context in which the example appears. In this example the first violins are the only ones to have quintuplets. If the conductor were to beat in five, the rest of the orchestra would not be able to play their parts. The best solution is either to rewrite or to have the conductor beat four with one hand and five with the other. This is not as impossible as it might sound: there are a few conductors who can do it, and we will discuss how in the chapter on conducting.

The Common Sense Rule

In the next problem, we need to find the speed of a dotted quarter:

♩ =100 ,   ♩. = ?

Just as the triplet quarter and the normal quarter did not relate directly, neither do the dotted quarter and the quarter. To solve this problem it will help to know another rule.

Students often come up with answers to speed problems that are far off the mark. This sometimes happens because they multiplied when they should have divided and vice versa. They can avoid this mistake by using the common sense rule: The larger the unit, the slower the metronomic speed; the smaller the unit, the faster the metronomic speed. In the above example, is the dotted quarter larger or smaller than the quarter? Obviously it is larger, which tells us that the metronomic speed must be slower. The rule does not give the answer; it only shows if the student has gone the wrong way.

Let us return to the problem of the dotted quarter. Dotted notes can be considered a family, and the first step in relating different families is to find a common unit. Since normal notes and dotted notes, unlike bracket families, are made up of the same smaller units, we will not be looking for a common unit from the dotted family. Instead we will look for the largest normal value that fits into both the normal quarter and the dotted quarter. This is the eighth: a normal quarter contains two eighths, and a dotted quarter contains three. We then find the speed of the eighth by multiplying 100 by two and get 200. The dotted quarter contains three eighths, so to get its speed we divide 200 by three and get 66.6. The common sense rule confirms that mm 66.6 can be the right answer: since a dotted quarter is larger than a normal quarter, its speed must be slower. If we had *multiplied* 200 by three and got mm 600, the rule would have told us that our answer was wrong: the dotted quarter cannot be faster than a normal quarter..

Here are a few examples for practice. In all of them a normal quarter = mm 84. Calculate the speed of other notes.

A normal thirty-second note: There are eight thirty-seconds in a quarter: 8×84 = 672.

One triplet half note:

Large method: Complete the bracket with similar values:

Three triplet half notes are in the space of two normal half notes, which equal a whole note. The whole note has a speed of mm 21 ($84 \div 4$). There are three triplet half notes in the whole note; $3 \times 21 = 63$.

Small method: Find the largest triplet unit that fits into the triplet half and a normal quarter. The answer is a triplet eighth. Therefore the speed of one triplet eighth is $3 \times 84 = 252$. The equivalency rule says that there are four triplet eighths in a triplet half: $252 \div 4 = 63$.

A quintuplet eighth:

Complete the bracket. Five eighths are in the space of four normal eighths, which equals a half note. The speed of a half note is mm 42 ($84 \div 2$). There are five quintuplet eighths in a half note, so the speed of a single quintuplet eighth is $5 \times 42 = 210$.

A dotted sixteenth: The common unit is thirty-seconds rather than sixteenths because a sixteenth does not fit into a dotted sixteenth. The speed of a thirty-second is found by multiplying 84 by eight, which equals 672. The dotted sixteenth contains three thirty-seconds: $672 \div 3 = 224$.

A septuplet quarter:

Large method: Complete the bracket. Seven in the space of four quarters equals a whole note, and the speed of a whole note is mm 21 ($84 \div 4$). There are seven septuplet quarters in the whole note: $7 \times 21 = 147$. It should be noted that there are other ways to complete the bracket, which if used to find the answer will give the same result:

Small method: A septuplet sixteenth fits both a normal quarter and a septuplet quarter. The speed of a septuplet sixteenth is $84 \times 7 = 588$. The equivalency rule tells us that there are four septuplet sixteenths in a septuplet quarter: $588 \div 4 = 147$.

Here are the first three measures of a work by Luigi Dallapiccola:

We need the metronomic speed of one of the bracketed eighth notes in each measure (as shown by the arrows). This problem could have been stated in the same manner as the others, but it is instructive to see how it actually appears in the music. Incidentally, the passage is a unison for the whole group of players, presumably while the conductor is conducting in two—a rather simple mechanical task for the conductor. But the conductor must be able to ascertain if the players are correct, and if not, to teach them how to play it.

Before working on the problem, one might have a look at the three measures and try to guess which set of eighth notes is the fastest, which is the second-fastest, and which is the slowest.

The first bracket is over six normal eighths, or three quarters, which we can also call a dotted half note. We find the speed of the dotted half by dividing the quarter speed, 120, by three and get 40. We then multiply the speed of the dotted half by seven and get the answer, *280.*

The second bracket is over a half note, whose speed is mm 60. Five times 60 is *300.*

The third bracket is also over a half note, which contains six triplet eighths. Six times 60 equals *360.*

The next problem involves the mixing of families (bracketed notes):

DOUBLE CONCERTO FOR HARPSICHORD, PIANO AND TWO CHAMBER ORCHESTRAS, by Elliot Carter. Copyright © 1964 Associated Music Publishers, Inc. International Copyright Secured. All Rights Reserved. Used by Permission.

As might be expected, we will need the largest unit that is common to the eighth and the triplet eighth: namely, a triplet sixteenth. The eighth contains three, and the triplet eighth contains two, for a total of five triplet sixteenths. The speed of a triplet sixteenth is 105 × 6 (there are six triplet sixteenths in a quarter) = 630. Divide this by five to get mm 126 for the new quarter.

Here is a chart showing a comparison of metronomic speeds of the most common families. They are all in terms of a normal quarter equaling mm 100:

NORMAL	TRIPLET	(5:4) QUINTUPLET	(7:4) SEPTUPLET	DOTTED
o =25	o =37.5	o =31.25	o =43.75	o· =16.6
♩=50	♩=75	♩=62.5	♩=87.5	♩.=33.3
♩ =100	♩ =150	♩ =125	♩ =175	♩. =66.6
♪=200	♪=300	♪=250	♪=350	♪.=133.3
♬=400	♬=600	♬=500	♬=700	♬.=266.6

♩=100

Metric Modulation

Mathematical manipulation has always been inherent in the rhythmic structure of music, but only in the twentieth century has it become a coherent compositional tool. A group of composers who have developed the techniques of Arnold Schoenberg and Anton Webern use mathematical manipulation in a simplistic way to order and reorder a series of pitches and other musical parameters. This is done, for example, by assigning numbers to sets of pitches and then manipulating the numbers in various ways. By contrast, metric modulation, developed by the American composer Elliott Carter, is a much more complicated technique. It is directly related to the types of performance problems with which we are concerned.

The term *modulation* immediately brings to mind the subject of harmony. Harmonic modulation, which in its classical usage was a method for moving from one key to another, always involved a common or pivotal chord that existed in both the old and the new key. This chord served one harmonic function in the old key and a different harmonic function in the new one. It acted as a bridge between the two tonalities so that the transition was both smooth and logical, even if it often surprised the listener.

Metric modulation is a technique for shifting from one tempo to another. As it was first developed, it was similar to harmonic modulation in that something had to be common to both tempos—a metric unit that proceeded at the same speed in both tempos. Let us look at an early use (J. S. Bach) of the same technique in its most basic form, long before it was called metric modulation:

Here we have a slow introduction followed by an allegro. Typically at the end of the movement there would be a return to the slow tempo. It has become traditional for the allegro to be performed twice as fast as the introduction, even though this is not specifically stated. It is simply a natural way of relating the two tempos. Of course, one does not have to play the allegro twice as fast, but most musicians probably would. At a later time composers started using the Italian words *doppio piu mosso,* or *doppio piu lento,* to mean either twice as fast or twice as slow.

Still later some composers adopted the following notation:

(Adagio) ♩ = ♪ (Allegro)

This meant that the quarter in the allegro measure should go at the speed of the eighth in the adagio (introduction), or twice as fast. A doubling or even a tripling of the tempo was shown, but nothing more complicated than that. The notation shown above was used into the twentieth century until metric modulation became established. A new notation for the metric modulation itself was formulated that reversed the older notation:

♪ = ♩

This was very logical in that each rhythmic quantity appeared over the measure in which it existed.

If metric modulation only dealt with such simple relations, there would be no need for the system. However, the relations have become more and more complicated and obscure. Let us start, though, by examining a type of metric modulation that is still fairly simple:

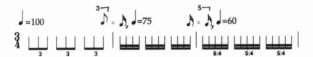

The most significant feature of these modulations is that the subdivided units in all of the measures are at the same speed. This is indicated by the legend that appears between each measure telling us that the subdivided unit in one measure is equal to the one in the next measure. Each unit is at a speed of mm 300: in the first measure the quarter = 100, triplet eighth = 300. This results in the inner units continuing unchanged from measure to measure while the larger beat changes. We are told to what speed the quarter changes (though we have learned how to figure out the speed should the composer not provide the information). Let's look at a few metric modulation problems:

A

$\quad \math質=50 \qquad$ 7:4

B

$\quad =72 \qquad$ 5:4

C

$\quad =95 \qquad$ 5:4 3

D

$\quad =60 \qquad$ 3 7:4 $\qquad =25.7$

There are several other ways of showing the quantity seen in example A, which is three septuplet sixteenths:

7:4   7:4   7:4   7:4

All are in use, although there may be some confusion concerning the rests, which are not really a part of the quantity under discussion. The unit is a dotted eighth septuplet, or three septuplet sixteenths tied together. To find the answer, we first get the speed of a single septuplet sixteenth: $7 \times 50 = 350$. To find the speed of the dotted eighth, we divide 350 by three and get *116 2/3*. This is the speed of the new quarter. Do not be surprised to see fractions: they are a natural part of this kind of metric manipulation. No one supposes that a musician could pick out a tempo with a fraction. But in fact no musician can pick out any speed exactly, except by chance. Ask ten musicians to beat mm 60, probably the most familiar speed, and you will receive ten different answers. A musician who is well trained in rhythms, though, can always come close to the desired speed. The purpose of metric modulation is to produce the *correct relation* between two speeds rather than the exact metronomic speed of each.

To solve example B by the large method, we fill in the bracket with quintuplet eighths—five in the space of four, written as 5:4, which equals a normal half note. The speed of a normal half is found by dividing 72 by two to get 36. Five times 36 gives us the speed of one quintuplet eighth: mm 180. Therefore 180 is the speed of the new sixteenth, and to find the new quarter we divide it by four and get *45*.

Example C is similar to B, but in this case let's follow the small method. The speed of a quintuplet sixteenth is $95 \times 5 = 475$. By the equivalency rule we know that the speed of a triplet eighth must also be mm 475. The normal quarter has three triplet eighths in it, so we divide 475 by three and get *158*.

Example D: The speed of the triplet eighth is $60 \times 3 = 180$. Therefore the new septuplet sixteenth is also mm 180. The speed of the new quarter is found by dividing 180 by seven to get *25.7*.

A variety of problems arise when performing the various types of metric modulations. One involves a continuous series of fast notes grouped differently on each side of the modulation:

The difficulty is in working with a fast stream of notes and being able to place them into any size of group. The kind of practicing necessary for this will be discussed later in this chapter.

Another type of modulation has the inner units on only one side of the modulation:

Here the performer has to continue them mentally until the new tempo has been established.

In a third type the inner units are not played, but they are used to establish the modulation:

Here the inner units (quintuplet sixteenths) must be in the performer's mind before the modulation.

Most composers would agree that metric modulation came into being primarily as a way of relating tempos. To do this properly requires the performer to understand the difference between accuracy and flow, the difference being crucial to the performance of all music.

Flow versus Accuracy

The term *flow* and *accuracy* are in every sense opposites. The one cancels the other. Even though flow is very hard to define, all good musicians understand it, even if only instinctively. Accuracy, on the other hand, is very easy to define: every rhythm in its precise place. That is easier said than done, and in reality only a machine can accomplish it perfectly. But that is just as well, because when a person plays absolutely accurately the performance can sound too machine-like.

The important issue is to know when the music requires accuracy and when it requires flow. It is ultimately an interpretive decision on the part of the performer, although often a composer will write above a passage *rubato,* or *freely,* to indicate that flow, not accuracy, is paramount. The difficult thing for people who do not understand this concept is that the change from one to the other can occur even from measure to measure. Obviously, accuracy does have a crucial role in music, and metric modulation in particular requires a high degree of accuracy if the correct tempo relations are to be maintained.

We usually think of flow in terms of a liquid. All liquids flow, whether thick or thin, and they do this smoothly. In flowing around an object a liquid may speed up or slow down, but will never lose its coherence. In music this could be likened to the change in speed of the musical flow at an important note or harmony. Because of the slowing down or speeding up, flow also implies a degree of rubato. Rubato is the altering of the length of notes to reflect a certain emotional significance. This type of heightening can result in notes being stretched far beyond what the metric notation seems to call for. Extreme use of rubato is often found in opera and instrumental concertos, especially from the romantic period.

All of this does not mean that music played with flow or rubato is simply inaccurate; it does mean that there is a temporal give and take that follows the expressive intent of the music. Speech goes through a similar process of inflection and punctuation to bring out important words and ideas. In music the heightening and stressing is done by altering the timing or volume of a single note or a series of notes.

Imitating Natural Accents

How does this discussion of flow apply to metric modulation, which seems to call for complete accuracy? First let us look at a basic rhythm:

No one would think of gathering the sixteenths into a single group of twelve or separating them into twelve ones. The notation itself shows us that they are grouped into fours on each beat. They flow this way, with the slightest accent on the first sixteenth of each group, which we unconsciously think of and call *one* (*one*-two-three-four, *one*-two-three-four, etc.). Let us now add another rhythmic configuration to this one:

It is easy to see that the composer wanted the feeling of two different meters at the same time: 3/4 and 12/16. The written meter is 3/4, while 12/16 (three on a beat) is produced artificially by the accents. Now if the player of the bottom line should actually try to play three notes on a beat, as if it were actually in 12/16, instead of playing the passage as a syncopation, there is little chance of the two players' staying together. The downbeat feeling of the threes would inevitably produce a different flow, causing the sixteenths to be at a different speed. It is not possible to be in the world of three and the world of four at the same time.

This discussion is from the point of view of the player because things are very different for the listener, who is not tied to the beat. The listener can be led to hear the passage as either a syncopation or a separate meter, which way depends on how much accent the player applies. Usually, the more accent, the more the syncopated aspect is emphasized, because the conscious degree of accenting is likely to go beyond the subtle degree of stressing in a true 12/16 meter. The performer will always experience the passage as being syncopated because of being locked into the 3/4 beat, but the listener could experience it either way.

This situation is by no means unique to twentieth-century music, as the following example from Brahms's Third Symphony demonstrates:

The meter here is 6/4, a duple meter, whereas some of the movement is notated in 3/2, a triple meter. This rhythmic shifting occurs again and again throughout the symphony and is characteristic of Brahms's music. The key to performing this example and others like it is first an understanding of this duality, then a determination of whether or not to accent, and how much.

Let's look at the opening of the symphony (next page). Should it sound like 6/4 or 3/2? If we respect Brahms's notation in 6/4, we might want it to sound syncopated. There are, however, a few conductors who disagree with this and actually conduct the opening in 3/2. This results in a smoother flow in three, with much less harshness and energy of attack. The meter that is chosen would force the phrase to sound one way or the other. Brahms's works are full of "artificially" created meters and downbeats. An example from Brahms's First Symphony (pp. 59–60) shows the downbeat's being displaced for many measures, to the point where the listener could forget that it has been displaced:

Brahms, Symphony No. 3, first movement

Brahms, Symphony No. 1, fourth movement

(continued on next page)

(*continued from p. 59*)

Music feels, sounds, and flows differently depending on whether one is playing with or against the beat. Here is another example, from Beethoven's Third Symphony:

3/2 and 6/4 Compared

The 3/2 and 6/4 meters are often confused. In the next example, we see exactly the same rhythmic configuration in 6/4 and 3/2:

There are many other rhythmic configurations which would look the same in both meters. Remember, though, that 3/2 is a triple meter and 6/4 a duple meter, meaning that 3/2 will have three main stresses and 6/4 will have two. 6/4 (and 6/8) is essentially a subdivided meter, with each main beat subdivided into three. Of course, when the tempo is fast, one does not actually subdivide. On the other hand, if the music were written without any of the smaller units, there would be no reason not to call it 2/2 or 2/4. The situation is a little different for 3/2 because although a particular piece may only use half notes, the choice of 3/2 also tells us something about the tempo and suggests that the music should sound majestic. Many important composers have used these meters interchangeably when in fact they are not interchangeable, and have thus done a disservice to their own music.

Consider the following metric modulation:

In the first measure the groups of four sixteenths have their normal flow. In going from one measure to the next, the first task is to make sure that the speed of the inner units does not change, or else the metric relationship will not be the one the composer has asked for.

To keep the sixteenths at exactly the same speed is a mechanical operation requiring precision and accuracy. This kind of mechanical precision is best produced by a metronome set to the speed of the sixteenths—a metronome will not change speed as the music goes over the bar line. Human performers can never be this objectively accurate, though they can learn to achieve a high degree of accuracy. In the present example the normal flow of four on a beat will have been established by this point in the music, but it must be altered shortly before the modulation. Instead of feeling four on a beat, we shall have to imagine each individual note, especially when crossing the bar line. That there are three notes on a beat should only be established after making sure that the speed of the individual notes has not been changed. Then the normal three flow can take over.

This procedure is also necessary for the next example because the twos feel so unlike the threes that great care must be taken to assure that the speed does not change.

The next example takes us a step further:

There are two choices for how to handle this problem. Most musicians would treat it as a cross-rhythm, because that is the way the modulation reads: triplet quarter equals normal quarter. This requires the player to imagine (and play) three against two before the modulation and then go on with the same quarter-note triplet speed afterward. What makes the execution tricky is that the cross-rhythm is by definition three *against* two. The triplet quarters are at first against the two normal ones, and in example B they have been rewritten to be compatible with the normal notes. When those normal quarters disappear, there is nothing for the former triplets to be against, and because of this there is a strong possibility that their speed will change. Many students feel when they first try this that they have suddenly lost their anchor and are guessing at the correct speed.

There is a technique for accomplishing this type of transition that can be developed and used for all similar problems. It requires the player to be both a performer and a listener. While performing the cross-rhythm, the player should at the same time listen to the triplet notes and hear them as an independent speed of note. They must be heard apart from the formal time signature of the measure, the way a listener would perceive them. Then the speed of note can be continued on its own into the next measure.

Here is another example for additional practice in this technique:

The metric modulation could have been written as follows:

We can see that these are equivalent because the final rewriting would show that each of the four quarters (of the 4×3) would consist of a value three sixteenths long, or a dotted eighth. To practice this, set the metronome to the speed of the normal quarters of the 3/4 measure. Then play or tap four against three for a few measures. When this feels secure, the four should then be listened to independently of the cross-rhythm. At this point the metronome should be turned off and the fours continued as an independent tempo, which will also be the correct tempo.

The other method for solving the problem shown on p. 63 relies on our realizing that if a triplet quarter equals a normal quarter, then a triplet eighth = a normal eighth, a triplet half = a normal half, and so on. This second solution involves selecting the rhythmic unit that is both easiest to work with and most appropriate to the particular problem (the composer by no means always chooses the one that is most helpful to the performer). In this case the triplet eighth should be the inner unit, two of them at the bar line will give the speed of the new quarter. The performer should use whichever of these two solutions is most appropriate to the problem at hand.

In the following problem let us assume that the quintuplet quarters do not appear in the first measure:

Since they cannot be listened to, one must set up their speed mentally. This is always much harder for quintuplets than it is for triplets. The three methods of rewriting that can be used are:

Example A is the hardest because it requires setting up one of the more difficult cross-rhythms: 5×4. It can be done, but probably at the cost of too much effort.

Example B employs 5×2. This cross-rhythm is simpler than 5×4 but requires a further step: two of the quintuplet eighths are needed to set up the new quarter. This would certainly work unless the new measure went on, for example, in the following way:

This situation leaves very little time to establish the new quarter before an additional rhythm has to be introduced. One way around this is to tie the last two quintuplet eighths mentally and try to keep the resultant quintuplet quarter in mind to set up the new speed.

Example C would be the easiest if the new measure continued with sixteenths, just as B would be easiest if the new measure continued with eighths. On the other hand, if it went on as in example D, rewriting in sixteenths would require that the last four quintuplet sixteenths be tied mentally to establish the speed of the new quarter. So we see that none of the three solutions is automatically the best. Each is adequate to a specific musical context, and performers will choose whatever they believe to be the easiest solution under the circumstances.

The next example is from the Double Concerto by Elliott Carter:

This passage has been discussed previously (p. 50) as a problem in metronome speeds. It is played by the oboe, and none of these rhythms appear anywhere else in the ensemble. The first measure is conducted in a pattern of 2+3, so the conductor can be of no particular help to the oboist without confusing the rest of the players. Most musicians, including conductors, will not realize that the oboe rhythm is exactly the same as the cross-rhythm 3×5, which could be shown as follows:

This also illustrates another way to find the speed of the new quarter should it not have been given. Notice in the original example that all of the notes are of exactly the same length: five triplet eighths.

To find the speed of the new quarter would require finding the speed of the entire 5/8 measure: quarter = mm 105, eighth = mm 210, and 210 ÷ 5 = 42. Since there are three notes during the time mm 42, the speed of the new quarter is 42 × 3 = 126.

Let us first examine the situation from the oboist's point of view. The conductor will be beating a quarter followed by a dotted quarter (2+3) because the speed of this passage, quarter = 105, would make it impractical for the conductor to beat eighths (at mm 210). This is not a problem in the first part of the measure because the oboe part fits quite well with a quarter beat. But the oboe part does not fit within the dotted quarter beat of the second part of the measure. There are two ways that the oboist can "count" this measure. One is to subdivide and use the eighths throughout. It is difficult to work with such fast units, but it can be done, although not smoothly. Then there is the additional problem of continuing at the speed of those three notes in the next measure. Another way of handling this problem involves listening to the speed of notes being produced independently of the particular counting procedure. In this case the first two notes are quite easy to play; and since it takes only two notes to establish a tempo, if one had listened to them objectively, then going on at that speed of note should not be too difficult. Of course it would also be prudent for the oboist to watch the conductor to be sure that they arrive at the next downbeat together.

From the conductor's point of view, it is only necessary to listen to the three notes in the same way that the oboist listened, then go on at that speed. Otherwise the conductor must make a guess in jumping from mm 105 to mm 126. It should be possible to guess with a fair degree of accuracy, but since the oboist is already playing at mm 126, it seems best for the conductor simply to follow the oboist's lead.

Carter, the main proponent of metrical modulation as a compositional technique, uses a different notational device in place of the explanatory bracket. Carter's bracket looks like this:

He uses the bracket this way because it is metrically correct, whereas the explanatory bracket is only correct because it pronounces itself correct. Most present-day composers use the explanatory bracket we have been using in this book, which shows the equivalent rhythmic values as the Carter example:

Let us compare the two notational methods by looking at a simpler version of the phrase:

The first measure is "correct" because the bracket tells us that it is correct: it reminds us that the four eighths are not normal eighths but rather are in the ratio of 4:3. Carter's version, on the other hand, is numerically precise; that is, there are exactly four dotted sixteenths, which also equal twelve thirty-seconds, in the measure, and it is easy to see that twelve thirty-seconds fit neatly into a 3/8 measure:

B

We see that disregarding the explanatory bracket there are too many sixteenths in the measure. If we imagine a septuplet on each eighth of the 3/8 measure, we would have the following:

A

There are twenty-one septuplet thirty-seconds in the measure. Carter's version also has twenty-one thirty-seconds in the measure, making it numerically correct:

B

The difficulties with this method have to do both with comprehension and with the question of flow versus accuracy. Concerning comprehension, many musicians would find the following example at least a little baffling:

It indicates that each dotted quarter, instead of the normal six sixteenths in a 6/8 measure, has four units on it (dotted sixteenths). Dotted rests can make it even more confusing. Most players would prefer to see this example written as:

As far as flow is concerned, dotted rhythms usually imply syncopation, or at least angularity and precise playing, except in meters that are composed of dotted rhythms, such as 9/16 or 12/16:

The lack of flow may or may not be what the composer had in mind. Some players might even try to count this example by subdividing as follows:

This way of counting would certainly be antithetical to playing with flow.

The dotted note system can be applied to only certain rhythmic situations. In such meters as 6/8, 9/8, and 5/8, for example, it allows even-numbered groupings to be used along with some of the odd-numbered groupings:

Most composers feel that consistency is the most important consideration in choosing a system, and therefore they will continue to use the explanatory brackets. But since Carter has been so influential in this area, the future may see his system come into general use.

Chapter 4
The Basics of Conducting

Conductors and instrumentalists face many of the same problems in dealing with twentieth-century music. The traditional
role of the conductor, which was to interpret the music for the
performers, has not changed. The developments in rhythmic
complexity, including rapidly changing meters and new notational systems, have meant that conductors must greatly expand
their technique. Although this book deals specifically with
twentieth-century music, it will first be necessary to go through
the fundamentals of conducting in order to see why and how the
techniques have expanded. Another reason is that the book is
intended for musicians and composers (as well as conductors)
who may not have had much training in conducting. This is
especially important since many of the ensembles devoted to
newer music are led by composers or by musicians in the ensembles.

Conducting Patterns
The most basic function of conducting is to show the meter and
tempo of the music to the performers, and this is done by means
of patterns of arm motion. The standard patterns for beating two,
three, and four have developed over the course of music history
and are universally accepted. Details may vary, but in general
they look like this:

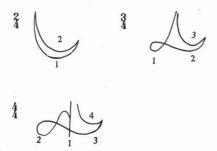

(These drawings are only rough approximations in two dimen-
sions of three-dimensional patterns.)

Until the twentieth century there were relatively few patterns to learn, and their execution was deceptively simple. Gradually, new meters were introduced, which called for altering the older patterns. In fact, all of the newer patterns, such as 5/8, 7/16, and 11/8, are directly related to one of the standard patterns. The only completely new pattern is for five independent beats. Independent beats are best understood by referring to a typical 4/4 measure, in which each beat has its place and none of them are grouped together, the way they would be in a 2/2 measure. A 2/2 measure groups two quarters on each beat, and to beat all four quarters a conductor would have to subdivide the two main beats rather than conducting the four independent beats of a 4/4 measure.

The pattern for five independent beats is:

This pattern can only be done if the tempo is slow to moderate. At faster tempos this meter is either done in one or is subdivided. There are virtually no meters larger than five that call for independent beats, no matter how slow the tempo. A striking exception is found in Stravinsky's *Le Sacre du Printemps,* where we find an 11/4 measure:

An important feature of the patterns on the previous page is that the downbeats go in different directions. Not all conductors agree about this, although the ones who disagree tend to conduct twentieth-century music only rarely. In the past, entire movements were often in one meter, and it did not matter where the conductor gave the downbeat because the players were never in doubt about where the downbeat went. With the advent of rapidly changing meter, it is a completely different story. The performers rely on the conductor to confirm which measure they are in. This confirmation happens if the players, on seeing the downbeat, know whether the measure is in two, three, or four beats. Obviously, if the downbeats for all the measures look the same, one cannot be sure which measure it is until the second beat takes place. By that time it can well be too late.

The audience often gets the impression that the players never look at the conductor. This is not true: they are always peripherally aware of the conductor, and do look up whenever something important is about to happen. Of course, they cannot do this as continually as a rapidly changing meter demands. This is another reason for distinct directions for the downbeats of the various meters, for if executed properly they will be noticed, even if only peripherally. This system of directions works for all the irregular meters, except for five independent beats. However, this occurs mainly in slower tempos and therefore is usually not a problem. It would not be possible to have a different direction for every meter because there would be confusion as the zones started to overlap. Three is the limit for recognition purposes. Of course, this system can and should be applied to older music, although the extremes of displacement are not as important.

Conducting patterns take place in space, and we should consider this space as a frame. The height and the width of the frame are not fixed, but will change depending particularly on the dynamics of the music. All members of the orchestra can easily see the height of the frame changing, but not the width. In the physical placement of the orchestra on the stage, we see that many of the string players (usually the first violins and the cellos) are grouped directly on both sides of the conductor. Their depth perception starts to disappear after ten or twelve feet, and unless the conducting pattern covers some degree of width, they are unable to distinguish one beat from another, particularly if they are only glancing up. A typical 4/4 beat, which looks perfectly fine from the front, may have nothing to distinguish the beats when viewed from the side:

$\frac{4}{4}$

Another important point about the frame concerns its base. The base is where the beat points fall. Therefore if the conductor alters the base too often, the players may have a hard time playing together.

The Mechanical Principles of Arm Motion

Why are some conductors easy to follow and others very difficult? The reasons have to do with the principles of arm motion. (The conductors who are difficult to follow usually stay away from twentieth-century music.) Some conductors even seem to make a virtue of being unclear; perhaps they feel it is a sign of deep involvement with the music. Whether it is or not, the music comes only through the performers, and they need to feel reasonably secure to make that happen. Vagueness of beat can play an important role in imparting a particular quality to the music. This is something that should be done consciously by the conductor. No matter how deep the musical thought, however, too much raggedness will destroy it.

An element of psychology, sometimes unconscious, may be behind a vague beat. For one thing, it may force the players to listen to each other, because otherwise they would not know where to place their notes. Players of course should always listen to one another and not rely solely on the conductor's beat, except in some twentieth-century music where none of the beats are audible. Secondly, vague attacks (particularly from the strings), imperceptible releases, and other such expressive devices are often the result of a conscious desire for less accuracy, which can be conveyed by the type of beat the conductor uses. The mechanical side of conducting consists of using the arm (or arms) to shape the patterns, and the time points for the beats not only must be shown but also must be predictable by the players. In one sense, conductors are always predicting the future by one beat.

The Beat

Conducting patterns are made up of straight lines and curves. The faster the tempo, the straighter the lines, although in going from one beat to the next the conductor almost always uses a curve. Here is a typical pattern for a 3/4 measure:

In most instances the downbeat will be the straightest line of all. Its terminus we shall call the *beat point*. For the beat point to be predictable, the players must know when it *will be* reached rather than know when it *was* reached. The earliest conductors gave the beat to the players by striking the floor with a wooden staff. The principle of striking something is familiar to everyone. It is a natural act that consists of accelerating the object that is doing the hitting until the moment of impact, when the energy dissipates; the object is then raised deliberately in preparation for the next strike. No one would think of driving a nail, for example, by moving the arm with the hammer up and down at a steady rate. Acceleration is the key to this natural act.

Strike a nail several times and notice what the arm does at the top of each stroke. In many ways this is like conducting one beat per measure at a tempo of, say, mm 84. At the top, the arm behaves like a ball thrown in the air. Does it stop before reversing itself? If it stops—and there is disagreement about this—it happens instantaneously. What is more, the ball decelerates until the moment of reversal. In baseball, the swing of the bat follows the same principles: an acceleration to the moment of impact, followed by the dissipating of energy. Another analogy with baseball and the prediction of the next beat is shown by the outfielder who almost immediately after seeing the ball struck knows where to run to catch it. He does this by noticing the trajectory and speed of the ball in its initial curve away from the bat:

An important principle about the curve of the beat can be seen by observing a pendulum. The beat point for the pendulum would be at the bottom of its swing, where it is traveling its fastest. From that point it slows down, instantaneously stops, reverses its direction, and descends for the next stroke. If we set a metronome to beat exactly with the pendulum, and then double the speed of the metronome so that it is beating duple subdivisions, we will notice that they occur at the exact moment when the pendulum stops and reverses itself:

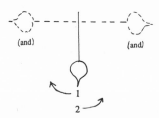

By analogy, the top of each curve of the conductor's beat should be reached at the same moment in time as would a duple subdivision:

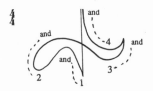

This is not the same as subdividing, and is not meant to be a precision movement. The moment in the beat that is being described consists of a continuously moving curve in which the upward motion imperceptibly stops and reverses itself:

A pendulum and a bouncing ball automatically produce these motions because after the initial push or throw, no forces act on them but gravity. The motion of a conductor's arm, however, is constantly being adjusted by the conductor, who controls it via the muscles and is thus able to resist the natural force of gravity. What we are trying to accomplish is to have the arm imitate the "naturalness" of the ball and pendulum. When patterns are done in this manner, they are extremely easy for the players to follow. Most conductors who are said to have good technique make use of these principles, whether they know it or not.

The acceleration to a time point predicts that point. There should be no motion from beat to beat without some degree of acceleration, except in rather rare instances. Going through a beat point without changing speed can only be done with very large curves, and these have only a vaguely outlined point:

It may well be that there is only one moment when the curve touches bottom, but since that moment is hard to see, the players will interpret the beat point differently. On the other hand, the following curves show the beats very clearly:

If, however, the music is going along steadily and the conductor is trying to avoid any hint of accent, then a beat that is more continuous and has bigger curves can be used. The conductor should be able to switch from broad curves to sharp lines as the occasion warrants. Put simply, curves equate with smoothness (flow), and straight lines equate with precision.

Conducting Irregular Meters

The irregular meters are those that combine twos and threes. The most obvious example is a 5/8 measure. We looked previously at the pattern for five independent beats, which occurs at slower tempos. Now let us consider much faster tempos, where it is impossible to conduct the individual eighths. A typical 5/8 measure is said to be a 2+3 measure, which means that the first beat (a quarter) contains two eighths and the second beat (a dotted quarter) contains three eighths:

It could also be a measure of 3+2. In either case, since there are two main beats, it is a duple measure and is therefore conducted in a two pattern. Another way of saying this is that if the measure is 2+3 then the first beat is the same as the first beat of a 2/4 measure, and the second beat is the same as the second beat of a 6/8 measure, with all of the eighths being at the same speed:

This is the single most important new pattern in the twentieth century, and it presents a special challenge to the conductor. It is not enough to be metrically accurate: one has also to show ahead of time where the next beat will fall. If one were to conduct a series of 2/4 measures at a speed of quarter = 112, each beat would have a natural curve and thereby predict the arrival point for the next beat. The same situation would prevail for the 6/8 measure done at dotted quarter = 76. The problem comes when we try to graft one onto the other.

Invariably, the beat that gives trouble is the dotted quarter. The underlying reason is that it is much slower than the quarter, and slower beats are always more difficult to convey accurately. The first prerequisite is that the inner eighths be at a constant speed. Then the curve for the dotted quarter must convey the next arrival point. In order to do this, it must be much larger than the quarter beat curve. If it is kept the same size, then the arm must slow down considerably to allow for the extra time the dotted quarter takes:

This is not easy to see. On the other hand, if the arm keeps the speed fairly similar for both beats but enlarges the motion for the dotted quarter, this is not only easy to see, but also alerts the players that it is a 5/8 measure:

A suddenly larger beat gets the attention of the players and can signal them that something different is about to happen. In general it is best to keep the beats for the irregular meters larger than the dynamic (volume of sound) might indicate, so that the arm does not have to move too slowly for the dotted quarter beat. This principle applies to all cases of twos and threes.

The Size of the Pattern

Most conductors and performers accept the idea that the larger the beat, the louder the dynamic. This concept works well because it is easy to see and respond to changes in the size of the beat. There have been famous conductors who refused to use this obvious technique and insisted that the musicians take on the responsibility for the dynamics. After all, the dynamics are written into the score by the composer, and the musicians should play what is in the score. Carried to its logical conclusion, this line of reasoning would say that conductors are not needed at all, since everything needed to perform the music is written into the score. Needless to say, I do not agree with this, although there are a few excellent ensembles who play without a conductor. The price for this, however, is a great deal of rehearsing. The best thing about this way of working, which is the rule for chamber music, is that it forces the players to know each other's parts, as well as their own—a noble idea that, unfortunately, given the time constraints under which we all labor, cannot work with a full symphony orchestra.

We can picture the dynamic range as being a series of frames of different sizes—a large frame, for instance, for fortissimo or a small one for pianissimo. The conductor beats within the frame, and the beats all land on the base of the frame. If we imagine a series of dynamic frames hanging on a wall, then the smaller the frame (the smaller the dynamic), the higher its base will be. Here is a useful exercise for dynamics and for the beat. First, find a surface at a convenient height—a solid music stand is good for this purpose (not a wire one). Then take a baton or a pencil and beat 4/4 measures so that each beat hits the surface. Even pianissimo dynamics should produce a fairly loud click. If this does not happen, then the idea of hitting the beat is not present. Remember, it is the hitting that positively locates the beat point. In loud dynamics, one should be hitting the surface quite sharply, and in actual conducting the conductor must create an imaginary surface and hit it just as forcefully. Since music often calls for sudden dynamic changes, one must develop the ability to change the size of the frame from beat to beat.

The Upbeat or Preparatory Beat

The single most important beat, and the one that causes conductors the most difficulty, is the upbeat. This is also the beat that gives the orchestra the most difficulty. At a concert, it is all too common for the first note of a work not to sound together. Every piece of music starts at a particular tempo, dynamic, and mood, and all of these parameters must be conveyed by the upbeat. Without exception, upbeats start from the right and go up in a curving motion:

The conductor must have the exact tempo in mind before giving the upbeat. Unfortunately, it is also common to hear a piece change tempo in the first measure, as the conductor realizes that it has not got going at the desired speed. Some conductors seem instinctively to know the speed they want and can start correctly without special mental preparation. Others have to take the time to imagine the speed before making the upbeat, often by mentally going through a few beats of the music.

Although I have been using the term *upbeat,* a more appropriate expression would be *preparatory beat.* In most pieces the music starts on the downbeat and therefore requires an upbeat. There are, however, innumerable examples that start on a different beat. The term *preparatory beat* can apply to all cases.

How many preparatory beats should be given? The answer depends mostly on the tempo of the work. All instrumentalists require a certain amount of time to prepare to play. The strings must get the bow in position and the fingering set, then have time to produce the desired stroke. The winds need to take a breath and set the embouchure. If the tempo is rather fast, one beat will not be enough time. A really fast tempo (quarter = 168 and above) could require three preparatory beats. On the other hand, really slow tempos certainly give enough time, but may have to be subdivided for accuracy.

Upbeats all look alike, but preparatory beats do not. A composer can start a piece, or a passage, on any beat of the measure. This means that the preparatory beat, assuming there is only one, must start on that part of the pattern that is one beat ahead of the music. If two are needed, then they start two beats ahead of the music.

Many beginning conductors, and even a few longtime professionals, have had the disconcerting experience of players' starting to play a beat before the conductor is expecting it. Obviously the conductor has done something to confuse them. This almost invariably has to do with the shape of the upbeat. Here is a picture of an upbeat, with the beat point marked:

Here are two additional examples of the same upbeat. Notice that although the beat points are the same, the points at which the conductor's arm starts are quite different:

In A, it is almost as high as the point where the downbeat starts, and in B, it is exactly at the beat point. Each of the three positions can elicit a different response, and two of these are not desirable. The players can easily mistake A for a downbeat, and they may all start too soon or, what is worse, only some of the players may start too soon. In other words, this upbeat has too large a downward component. Example B, on the other hand, has no downward component. This can lead to a lack of precision, because even though the upbeat started exactly at the beat point, that point could not be seen rhythmically by the players because the conductor never "hit" it. It also allows the players less time to prepare—a serious problem in fast tempos.

In addition to its critical role in establishing the tempo, the upbeat must also show the dynamics. The downbeat, on the other hand, is generally the most important beat to stress in the measure. Of course there are a great many exceptions to this, but unless the composer indicates otherwise, there should always be at least a degree of extra stress on the downbeat. This requires the upbeat to be a little larger, which the conductor accomplishes by raising the arm a bit higher than for the other beats. In general, then, we can consider the downbeat as a kind of rallying point for the players, one that is more and more necessary as rhythmic and metrical complications proliferate.

Subdividing and Grouping

Subdividing relates to slower tempos, whereas combining or grouping takes place with faster tempos. All meters can be subdivided or grouped depending on rhythmic or musical considerations. Here is a chart showing most of the possible subdivisions and groupings that may be used for the most common meters:

Chart for subdividing and combining

Time Signature	for slower tempos normal subdivided unit	for faster tempos normal larger unit	occasionally used	very rare
2/4	♪	♩	³ ♪	♪
3/4	♪	♩.	³ ♪	♪
4/4	♪	♩	³ ♪	♪ o
2/2	♩	o	♪	
6/8 9/8 12/8	♪	♩.	♩. (12/8)	♩. (6/8)
5/8	♪	♩, ♩; ♩♩. (in one)		
7/8	♪	♩, ♩.	♩♩♩. (in one)	

All of the meters built on quarters or halves are often subdivided, whereas all those built on eighths or smaller units are almost never subdivided. To depart from these norms would take an exceptional passage, such as this one from Anton Webern's *Six Pieces for Orchestra:*

SIX PIECES FOR ORCHESTRA, by Anton Webern. Copyright © 1956 by Universal Edition A.G., Wien. Copyright © Renewed. All Rights Reserved. Used by permission of European American Music Distributors Corporation, sole U.S. and Canadian agent for Universal Edition Vienna.

Because of the complexity of the rhythm and the need for perfect ensemble, this passage is best done by beating the slower sections in sixteenths.

In looking at the possible groupings for 6/8, we see that the dotted half is placed in the "rare" column because it would mean that the measure is in one. Only in very fast music would this be possible, such as this passage from Stravinsky's *Pulcinella:*

The flow of the music is in one, but this movement is extremely difficult and rhythmically intricate. Keeping the players exactly together is crucial to its performance, and if each and every one of them knew the music perfectly, it could probably be done in one. Yet this is often not the case. By beating dotted quarters, even though they are extremely fast, the conductor is giving the musicians twice as many reference points, which allows less wandering from the beat.

In more traditional music, the choice of meter conveyed the composer's intentions regarding subdivisions and stresses within the measure. For example, 2/4 and 4/8 may seem to be interchangeable, but this is not the case. 2/4 has two main stresses and, if it is slow enough, also has two minor stresses. Even in a slow tempo, 2/4 implies conducting in quarters. 4/8, on the other hand, implies four independent beats, in the same way that 4/4 does. A dilemma occurs for the conductor when the meter is 2/4, but the speed of the eighths is rather slow. A good example of this is seen in the slow movement of Beethoven's Third Symphony:

Marcia funebre.

Although the meter is 2/4, Beethoven gives the metronome speed of the eighth, implying that this is the unit that should be conducted. To conduct quarters at a speed of 40 could introduce a great many ensemble problems; but more important is Beethoven's indication of the eighth as the unit to work with. The question is what conducting pattern should be used: subdivided 2/4, or 4/8? The differences between them relate to the number of stresses in the measure. There is no question, however, that the 4/8 pattern is much more comfortable for the players and the conductor. A visual danger with subdivided 2/4 is that when the music requires all of the eighths to be beaten at the same size, the players may confuse one for the other. 4/8 is what most conductors choose, but they must be careful to avoid any unnecessary offbeat accents.

Subdivided Patterns

The first rule about subdivided patterns is that the placement of the main beats should not be altered. Most conductors agree with this rule, except where 6/8 or 6/4 is concerned. We can consider subdivisions as the offspring of the main beats, because physically they accompany them. They may be bigger or smaller, but they are in the same areas of the pattern. Here are several of the patterns:

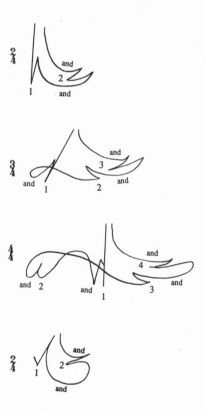

The subdivisions are shown in the size that would be used when the music is proceeding without sudden shifts in accentuation and dynamics. Of course, music does not always do that, and when required the size of the subdivisions must change. Often an offbeat, corresponding to a subdivision, will be more important than the main beat. This must be reflected in its size:

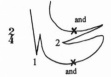

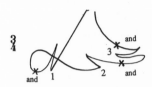

In the following example we have only loud offbeats, with rests on the main beats:

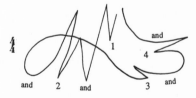

In this situation one must be careful not to give a big downbeat. A big downbeat is an invitation to play. Instead the pattern should look something like this:

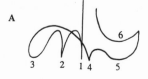

The invitation to play is the large curve after the downbeat that leads to the offbeat.

There are two standard 6/8 (or 6/4) patterns in use. They look like this:

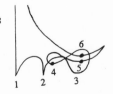

Of these patterns, B is by far the more useful because 6/8 is a duple meter and B is a duple pattern. All 6/8 meters that are not subdivided are done in a duple meter, which looks exactly like a 2/4 measure. Often in the same piece some measures are done in six and some in two. Pattern A requires an awkward switch from subdividing to not subdividing. In a gradual accelerando it will become necessary to switch from eighths to dotted quarters—again, awkward in pattern A. A useful technique in connection with pattern B and an accelerando is to phase out gradually the subdivisions as the dotted quarters take over. This is also impossible with pattern A:

There is a special type of subdividing that is done in slow music, when only certain beats (or measures) need greater accuracy. It violates the rule of not stopping the beat, but it works because the beat is stopped in a regularly recurring manner:

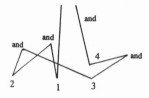

There is a definite rhythm for the stop-start motions. In this 4/4 measure, let us imagine a steady series of eighths. The motions are made at every eighth note, but pause on each before moving quickly to the next. The speed depends on the degree of accuracy desired; as this speed of the motion gets less and less, it starts to approach the nonsubdivided beat. It would be a good way of preparing for a sudden loud dynamic for the whole orchestra—say, on a downbeat. It can also be used to show a sudden change of tempo.

Sometimes a single passage of the music calls for subdivisions in some orchestral parts, but not in others. There are two methods of subdividing that satisfy both conditions. In one method, the subdivisions are kept extremely small, not necessarily because the dynamics are soft, but so that the players that do not need them can easily ignore those motions while the others can make use of them. It looks like this:

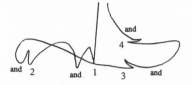

It is as if the arm were making the normal large motions while the hand shows the small subdivisions. The other method is to have the left hand follow the normal pattern while the right hand executes a smaller version with subdivisions.

Two Hands or One?

Traditionally the right hand is for keeping time and the left hand is for cuing and expression. There is still a good deal of truth to this, but things are not so clear-cut anymore. Most beginning conductors do not seem to know what to do with their left hand. One of the easiest options is to mirror what the right hand is doing, and this is very common. In fact,this technique does have its place and should not be banished, as many teachers would like. In older music, it was usually unnecessary because the musicians always could tell, if only by listening, where the beat was. As we have seen, this is not always the case in the twentieth century, and this way of conducting allows the peripherally placed groups of players to see the beat clearly. This technique should be used intentionally for that purpose, and not simply automatically to give the left hand something to do. When all of the difficult rhythms are occurring to the conductor's left, however, it makes perfect sense to use the left hand to mark the beat. Each hand should be capable of precision, expression, and cuing, but the primary responsibility for showing the beat remains with the right hand.

Conducting Two Meters at the Same Time

One of the earliest twentieth-century examples of two meters at the same time occurs in Stravinsky's *Petrouschka:*

B. & H. 16286

Basically, this is only a problem of three against two. Such a cross-rhythm usually does not need to have both meters shown since it is so familiar. Playing two quarters against three quarters is quite easy, but it becomes far more difficult when each of the three quarters has additional rhythmic units within it, as in this example. In order to play three against two it is necessary to work with the normal triplet eighths, but one cannot continue to do that when the internal rhythm becomes more complex. Hardly any conductors will bother or even be able to conduct both meters, and yet the passage is usually played with good ensemble. On the other hand, it is almost never played accurately in terms of what is actually notated. Maybe such accuracy is not necessary, but if a conductor wanted the passage to come out as Stravinsky notated it—and when played that way it has an audaciousness that is hard to achieve in any other way—then one has to conduct two against three. This makes it easy for the orchestra and hard for the conductor. Actually, the members of the orchestra see this kind of conducting so rarely that at first they may be confused about which hand to look at, but after the initial shock wears off they will have no problem with it. When the cellos enter they are first notated in 2/4, but in the next measure they are in 3/4. The first measure should be rewritten into 3/4 as well, because the change is awkward for them:

original: rewritten:

To go from a simple example to a complicated one, let us look at the last section of a work by Elliott Carter: the Double Concerto for Harpsichord and Piano with Two Chamber Orchestras (1961; see p. 90). In this work, the harpsichord and one of the chamber orchestras always play together, as do the other orchestra and the piano. Each group has its own melodic and rhythmic material. In the coda, which is several minutes long, the meter for Orchestra I is notated in 6/8, but since the material is mostly in 12/16 it should ideally be conducted in four. Orchestra II is clearly in 3/4. The rhythms within each group are so complicated that if only one meter was being conducted, the other group could not stay together. One solution, chosen by a few of the conductors who have done this work, is to alternate three and two (although four is better), depending on which group seems to need it more. This is only a halfway solution because there are too many times when both groups need to see the beat. Conducting four with the left hand (because Orchestra I is on the left side) and three with the right is the only way to achieve what Carter has

144

Coda

N. B.: From m. 619 to 653, the Percussion should slightly dominate the sonority without covering the soloists.

Dalla battuta 619 alla 653, la percussione deve leggermente predominare le sonorità senza sopraffare i solisti. Dei segni, nelle parti dei solisti, indiche-
ranno quando uno di essi deve predominare (l'altro solista avrà l'indicazione "accomp.").

written. An unusual problem that this solution creates is that when both hands are conducting, there is no way to turn the pages of the score! This involves careful planing to decide when to turn with each hand, or else one must memorize the whole section.

Carter's music contains many examples of the need to conduct two meters at the same time, as does the music of Charles Ives. The basis for conducting in two meters is the composite rhythm of the various cross-rhythms. In other words, the two meters must be tied to each other in this way. It is impossible to conduct two independent speeds at the same time with any degree of control. Therefore, a complete understanding of cross-rhythms is the first thing that the conductor of such works must undertake. One key is that the slower of the two beats is dependent on the faster beat. In most cases this is the workable solution. Unfortunately, there are cases where the slower beat is the first to show up in the music, and this is a more difficult situation to deal with.

An added difficulty is when the slow beat continues while the fast beat changes several times, as in this example from a work by Jeff Jones:

Here we have a continuing 4/4 time signature, against which is juxtaposed a 5/4 followed by a 7/4 (actually alternating measures of four and three), with enough different material to require both meters to be conducted along with the 4/4. An unusual solution is called for: namely, for the conductor to "observe" the 4/4 while changing from five to seven. This "observing" is a visual-physical act that is a bit hard to describe, but it involves letting the four beat float into the next measure, keeping aware of it, and placing the seven against it. (One only hopes there are no page turns.) This type of problem is still quite rare, but is really only an extension of the general difficulties with cross-rhythms.

Let's take an example from Ives's Fourth Symphony (facing page). Ives expected that three conductors would be required for this work because, besides various "normal" cross-rhythms, there are often several unrelated tempos going on at the same time. There are even accelerandos for one group while a steady beat goes on for another. Ives is definitely a visionary in the area of rhythmic independence, while still maintaining a high degree of control over vertical alignments. A more recent development, called spatial or aleatory music, aims for total independence, but at the cost of giving up all control over verticality. This kind of independence is easy to achieve since the choice of tempo is usually left to the individual players.

Some conductors take well to conducting two meters, while others find it beyond them. This is purely a problem of mechanics and coordination, and it does not reflect on one's musicianship. The easiest way to start developing the technique is by practicing with 2×3 (in a 3/4 measure):

1. Tap the cross-rhythm on a surface such as a table.
2. After this has been learned, raise the arms and tap in the air.
3. Beat a three pattern with the right hand, but continue the left hand as before.
4. Start to introduce a two pattern with the left hand.
5. Practice!
6. Practice!
7. Practice!

The main problem is getting the patterns to look as smooth as if each one were being conducted separately. Instead they tend to be erratic and jerky, with a series of straight lines instead of curves. If this happens, stop the three pattern and observe what a normal two looks and feels like. Then go back to conducting both. This will have to be repeated many times before it can look natural. The three will look good from the start, for it is always the slower beat that gives trouble.

The better one gets at doing these, the less energy will be required, allowing one to pay attention to the other important aspects of the music. All of the other techniques, such as those pertaining to dynamics and accentuation, may also be called for while there are cross-rhythms. Conducting two meters simultaneously should only be done when it is really necessary, because of the chance for confusion among the players.

Subdividing the Irregular Meters

Five-eight measures can be conducted in several different patterns. Two of them—all five eighth notes in one beat, and five independent beats—do not involve subdividing. There are several ways of subdividing fives, whether 5/8 or 5/4: 2+3, 3+2, or a combination of two twos and a one (2+2+1, 2+1+2, 1+2+2). The last three are only occasionally used, and they are all in triple meter (the same as the pattern for 3/4). The first two, 2+3 and 3+2, are both duple meters: that is, they have two main beats. The overall tempo will determine whether the beats are quarters and dotted quarters, or all eighths. In either case they are still duple measures. The patterns for the quarters and dotted quarters have already been discussed. The others look like this:

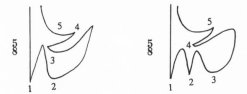

These are, of course, the subdivisions of a 2/4 and a 6/8 measure.

A useful pattern is based on 2+3, but has the three broken into a one and a two:

This can keep the rhythm tighter because it avoids the dotted quarter, which is always the beat that gives the most trouble. Also, in the following example, this pattern provides a quarter beat for the triplet, which makes it easier to play correctly. Of course, this would not be necessary if the conductor were to use a pattern of 3+2, but it is all too common in irregular meters for some of the rhythms to be 3+2, while at the same time others are definitely 2+3. The conductor must then make the decision as to which group needs the most help. The pattern we are now discussing is a good compromise and can help both rhythms.

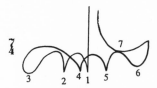

For 7/8, the normal groupings are two groups of two and one of three: 2+2+3, 2+3+2, and 3+2+2. These may be subdivided where all of the eighths are beaten, or just beaten as quarters and dotted quarters; but in all of these cases, the overall pattern is a triple one, with the same large pattern as 3/4. Occasionally, in faster tempos, we find 4+3 or 3+4, which calls for a duple pattern. It is extremely rare to find a one being used, but it would create a four pattern: 2+2+2+1. Seven-four is mainly used for slower tempos, but there is no adequate pattern for seven independent beats, which would require that each of the beats had its own distinct position and could not be confused with any other beat. We might imagine the following pattern, but we can also see the chance for confusion:

Seven broken down into 4+3 or 3+4 looks like this:

This is really a large duple subdivision.

The other subdivided patterns have to do with the following meters: 8/8, 9/8, 10/8, and 11/8. These meters indicate various groupings of two and three. 9/8, of course, will most often subdivide as 3+3+3. To decide on a pattern it is only necessary to see how many of these smaller groupings are called for, regardless of whether they are twos or threes:

4 patterns

(not triplets)

A meter of 8/8 theoretically means that there are two groups of three and a group of two. But 8/8 also conveniently falls into the normal four pattern, which is much easier to follow. Should the conductor always do what the composer has indicated, or do what is easiest for the players? The decision has to be based on the musical context and is by no means an automatic one. The next chapter will attempt to answer this question.

Chapter 5
Preparing the Score

No one would think of changing Beethoven's meters, bar lines, articulations, or rhythms, because he put them down in the best possible way to express his intentions. In the twentieth century, with its preoccupation with rhythmic and metrical complexities, many composers have not chosen as wisely.

The primary reason for any change must be to find an easier way to achieve what the composer has notated. In no way must a change result in altering the composer's intention. It is essential that the conductor analyze the situation properly: Does the composer want a syncopated feeling or a smooth one? Are the rhythmic complexities important to the passage, or do they just get in the way? Can the players manage the original, or would rewriting and rebarring the score help?

Let's look at a passage from Stravinsky's *Petrouschka* that is famous for causing conductors and orchestras great difficulty (see p. 98). Stravinsky uses 5/8 a great deal in his music, but is this passage really in 5/8? What pattern should the conductor use? The choices are 2+3, 3+2, and to beat the whole measure in one. None of these, however, represents what is happening in the music as a whole or in any of the parts.

The opening of the passage works well either in 2+3 or in one, but the rest is really in 3/4. When it is rebarred this way, it becomes quite easy to play, and without altering what Stravinsky wanted (see p. 99). Surely he did not intend for the players to get lost and have the passage fall apart, but that is what often happens. Notice that at the end of the passage it is necessary to introduce one 5/8 bar. This helps to establish the speed for the next section, because it seems that Stravinsky wanted the last quarter before the double bar to be at the same speed as the coming quarters. This can be accomplished by beating a 3+2 for the last bar but changing the speed of the last

quarter to correspond to the new quarter speed. The speed of the whole 5/8 measure is mm 72, which would make the quarter equal to mm 160—definitely not the new indication of quarter = 144.

What conducting pattern should be used for this *piu mosso* section? Since the previous section was at a quarter speed of 132, there is a definite tempo change at the 5/8. Seventy-two is a relatively low speed, which means that the players have no time at all to see what kind of a curve the conductor is projecting before they must make the decision as to how fast to play. A great deal of rehearsing would be required for all of them to chose the right tempo. Such guessing is not a comfortable way to make music. Conductors should seek more control, which they can get with a pattern of 2+3. Here the curve for the first quarter, at a speed of 160, would be fast enough to show the players the correct speed almost immediately. This places the responsibility for the correct speed on the conductor, where it belongs. If we look ahead eleven measures, however, we find that the 3/4 measure equals the previous 5/8 measure. A beat of 2+3 would not prepare the players for the much quicker eighths: 360 versus 432.

The best way to handle this problem is to go into a beat of one starting five measures before the 3/4. This is not difficult for the players because by that time the speed of the eighths is well established. Beating in one allows the players to gauge how fast to play the 3/4 measure. Right after the 3/4 measure, the beat should return to 2+3 in preparation for the rebarring into 3/4, at a quarter speed of 160.

Sometimes the composer manages to get the same effect as rebarring by means of articulation or stresses. It is then up to the conductor to understand what is happening and decide on the degree of stress. The next example, from *Mathis der Maler* by Paul Hindemith, has phrase lengths of many different sizes, all set into one meter. Hindemith has delineated the phrases with bowing indications, and the conductor must decide whether to make the changes in bowing stand out for the listener. Usually one is aware of them only in a subtle way, and this may be all that Hindemith wanted. But if the conductor thinks there should be more delineation, then the strings must emphasize the changes of bow. Writing in all the changes of meter would be going too far in this instance.

Earlier we examined the following example in terms of rewriting:

Here the conductor had to beat the measure in five because the players who did not have the triplet passage needed the conductor's normal beating pattern. However, if there was nothing else happening, then the simplest solution would be to move the bar line one eighth ahead by adding the first eighth of the measure to the previous measure. If this does not work because of some rhythmic complication in the previous measure, the pattern could start with a single eighth, then a normal 4/4 conducting pattern followed by another single eighth.

The following two passages, from Stravinsky's *L'Histoire du Soldat,* and Copland's *Appalachian Spring,* show that changing a meter can make things much easier for the players:

Three-four and 6/8 both contain six eighth notes, but the normal accentuation is different. This difference is important when the music is slower and more lyrical. In these examples, however, the most important thing is accuracy. The Stravinsky example is a 6/8 measure, which for the sake of accuracy is best done as 3/4.

The next two examples are from *Le Marteau sans Maître* by Pierre Boulez:

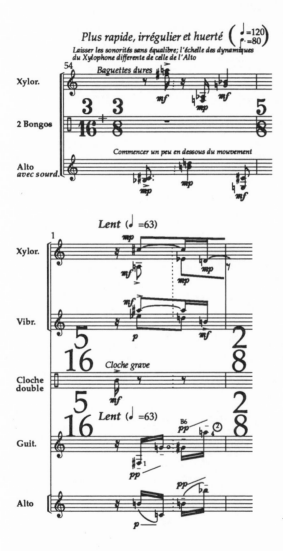

LE MARTEAU SANS MAITRE, by Pierre Boulez. Copyright © 1954 by Universal Edition (London), Ltd., London. Final Version: Copyright © 1957 by Universal Edition (London), Ltd., London. Poemes de Rene Char: Copyright © 1964 by Jose Corti, Editeur, Paris. All Rights Reserved. Used by permission of European American Music Distributors Corporation, sole U.S. and Canadian agent for Universal Edition London.

The first example occurs in the middle of the second movement, after a pause. It is called a 3/16 measure because Boulez's highly structured methods of composition probably called for a 3/16 measure at this point. The difficulty caused by having to change from 3/16 to 3/8 is completely unnecessary because although it is a 3/16 measure for the eye, it is not so for the ear. In addition, the speed and accents make the idea of any natural shaping of the measure meaningless. The measure starts out of silence, so that conducting this as a 3/8 measure does not add any unwanted silence and makes the transition to the next measure quite easy:

The second example is from the fourth movement. The single sixteenth is isolated, again after a pause, and contributes nothing to a 5/16 shape, while the rest of the measure is clearly in 2/8. Therefore the preparatory beats should also be in 2/8, with the written sixteenth being the last sixteenth of a new 2/8 measure.

Cross-rhythms present another choice for the conductor. How should the following example be conducted?

It can of course be conducted in four, which leaves all the problems to the players. Even when rewritten it is difficult to play. The best solution here is for the conductor to conduct in seven at the proper speed. This places the responsibility on the conductor, who must be able to jump accurately from mm 60 to mm 105. There are two ways to accomplish the jump. One is to take an educated guess at the new speed. The other way involves a metric modulation: in the measure before the seven appears, the conductor would imagine septuplet sixteenths in the last beat or so, then use four of them to provide the new septuplet quarter beat:

There is one other method, which is the only way to handle the problem if seven and four should happen at the same time, but this involves conducting seven against four. In some cases, this technique is the only one that will work.

Fermata

Two standard rules of conducting are that the arm should remain in constant motion, and that there should be only one downbeat in a measure and only one of each of the other beats. Both of these rules are often broken where fermatas are concerned.

The reason for the first rule is that whenever the arm stops there is no way for the players to know when it will start again. Occasionally a conductor will stop beating to heighten a dramatic effect. This will always get the players' attention (and the audience's), because they will be concerned about the next beat. But this should be used sparingly, with full knowledge of its purpose, and rarely in a difficult rhythmic situation.

When the beat stops, so does the rhythm. This of course is the intent of a fermata—to erase any sense of the beat. (I am speaking now about fermatas that occur during a piece, not at the end.) A fermata that contains a specific number of the ongoing rhythmic units is only partly fulfilling its purpose. Sometimes this kind of quantifying of the fermata works well, and sometimes not. It is certainly easier for everyone if the beat is felt during the fermata, but is this serving the composer's intent?

One of the ongoing questions concerns what happens after the fermata. Is there silence or not? The prototypical example is found at the beginning of Beethoven's Fifth Symphony:

Almost all conductors perform this as follows:

A few perform it this way:

And on rare occasions it is performed this way:

Which is "right"? Obviously Beethoven's choice was the "right" one, but no one can know exactly what was in his mind, and the notation does not settle the matter because musicians do not agree on how to interpret it. No rests are indicated, yet we are accustomed to hearing the passage played with them. Is this the voice of tradition, or is it a lack of technique? The argument will not be settled here, but certain conducting problems can unduly influence a conductor's choice of interpretation. Nothing that one does in music should be because of a lack of technique, and only when technique has been mastered is one able to choose objectively.

The first example is the easiest to perform because the beat, which is in one, can continue after the fermata and act as both a cutoff and an upbeat. This forces the one-measure silence, since no motion of the conductor is less than one measure long. The physical actions are as follows:

1. Start with a whole measure upbeat.
2. Keep the arm down on the fermata.
3. Give a whole measure upbeat as preparation for the cutoff.
4. Repeat 1–3.

Some conductors feel that the extra measure before the second fermata should be conducted since it is there. At least, this fermata should be longer than the first. If you conduct the extra measure, do not give a particularly large beat for the fermata itself, or some players may play the next measure. A provocative beat, when nothing is happening, is usually a bad idea.

In the second example, the conductor is trying to achieve what appears in the music, which is only an eighth of silence. This is both more difficult to convey and more awkward to play because there is hardly any time for bowing or breathing, but it can certainly be done. The steps are the same as for the first example except one: during the fermata, raise the arm *slowly* so as not to provoke a cutoff, but at a certain point make the upbeat suddenly as fast as the first upbeat in order to show the tempo.

The third example is a cross between the other two. It tries to reconcile their alleged discrepancies—that is, the notation that shows no rest, and the problem of preparation. It does this by splitting the difference and having only one quarter of silence. This is technically more difficult than the other methods. At the fermata, come up slowly , as in the second example; but at a certain point make a sharp cutoff (upbeat) the length of a quarter, then go on in one again.

A further refinement might be to go on after the second fermata with a one-measure rest because this fermata is longer. Most fermatas present the conductor with various choices like these. Just remember that it is always necessary to give a preparation for continuing, whether or not the continuing tempo is the same as before the fermata or different. Often the cutoff will be used as that preparation.

Next let us look at a typical fermata problem in the last movement of *Mathis der Maler.* This movement, particularly in the introduction, has problems relating to fermatas, organization of measures, and two-handed conducting. Here is the first example:

MATHIS DER MALER, by Paul Hindemith. Copyright © B. Schott's Soehne, Mainz, 1934. Copyright Renewed. All Rights Reserved. Used by permission of European American Music Distributors Corporation, sole U.S. and Canadian agent for B. Schott's Soehne.

The fermata is notated on the third beat of the measure, and the piece continues at a slightly slower tempo. How should the conductor's pattern look? The passage before the fermata ends with a loud dynamic, which needs a sharp cutoff. The tempo becomes an important factor, since the dotted quarter is at mm 176, making the eighth a meaningless quantity to work with at a speed of mm 528. There is an old rule of thumb that a fermata should be at least one and a half times longer than its written value, although this usually refers to slower tempos. In this case the fermata may turn out to be five or ten times as long, and if we look at the double bass or cello part, we see that the fermata is placed on a dotted quarter rest. In fact, it is unlikely that any conductor will stop on the third beat as indicated. This would allow no preparation for continuing without first going back and giving the third beat a second time. (In general, giving a beat more than once is to be avoided, although we will soon look at examples for which there are no other alternatives.)

In the present example, then, the fermata properly belongs on the rest of the second beat:

If the conductor were to try to have the fermata actually be on the third beat, as notated, he or she would then have to continue from this point. There would then have to be an instantaneous upbeat, which would allow the players almost no time to be prepared to play the upbeat note, let alone know what the new tempo is supposed to be.

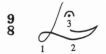

This type of beat is unhelpful. It is much better if the conductor thinks of the cutoff and fermata as being the second beat of the measure, after which there would normally be a continuation of the curve, which acts as a preparation for the third beat. It is like a freeze frame in cinema, after which the action continues. The continuation must not, however, be aggressive until the actual upbeat is reached or it may provoke too early an entrance. One does not want to give strong beats where nothing is happening except when trying to elicit a loud offbeat from a silent main beat.

The following example shows how an instantaneous beat might be used to good effect:

This example also illustrates the principle of not giving more preparatory beats than are necessary. At this tempo, only one preparatory beat should be given, and it must not be provocative. In other words, it should not be a loud beat. The instantaneous beat can be used since it does not allow the players time to come in, but does gives them the tempo:

Notice that the downbeat is small, but immediately grows to indicate the forte.

Another Hindemith example is at the beginning of the third movement:

The 4/4 measure appears to contain many more than four beats, and they all occur where the second beat would normally fall. In addition, the beamed notes are marked *rubato*. These notes must be grouped in some way, and since Hindemith has not done so, it is up to the conductor. That Hindemith has given the conductor the license to make such decisions is shown by the phrase *frei im Zeitmass* (free in tempo). Hindemith has helped only to the extent of putting dashes on the first three eighths, thus indicating that they are to be played more heavily (and probably more slowly) than the others. There are a total of nine notes under the beam, and they could be grouped in many different ways. Rather than go through all of them, let us consider just one, which will put them into a submeasure of 9/8, conducted as 2+2+2+3. This violates the rule calling for no more than one downbeat in a measure, unless all of those beats are given as a subdivision of the second normal beat. This is hard to illustrate because the subdivisions would fall mostly on each other, rather as they do when conducting all the eighths in a 9/8 measure:

After the subdivisions on the second beat the third normal beat takes over, and now the decision is whether to subdivide the rest of the passage in eighths. Most of it goes well in eighths, but what about the triplet in the second measure? Triplets and quintuplets longer than a normal quarter note are often kept more in line by subdividing than not, because subdividing predicts the next quarter beat more definitely. This would also allow a speed change to be more easily transmitted. The size of the subdivisions need not be large. Of course, one could always do the whole passage (after the nine eighth notes) in quarters. This depends on how much rubato is desired and on how good the orchestra is: the better the players are, the less extraneous help they need.

The next few measures contain some seemingly complicated rhythms:

The differences between the triplet sixteenths and the quintuplet sixteenths, and again between them and the septuplet sixteenths, is awkward to realize in performance. On the other hand, trying to play all of this precisely would go against the spirit of the markings *rubato* and *frei*. Many conductors recognize this and play the notes as groups of seven in the first case, nine in the second, with or without subdividing, and probably with some accelerando.

Rehearsal number 1 has an additional difficulty because of the trombones, cellos, and double basses:

If the upbeat to number 1 is done as a quarter and the conductor stops on the first fermata, those players on the second eighth will have trouble entering together. This is even more true if the conductor is giving fast subdivisions on the upbeat. Here is a good place for the right hand to conduct the measure (except for the dynamics) in the same way as the opening, while the left hand brings in the other players at the proper time.

In the last measure of the introduction there is another fermata, which leads into the *sehr lebhaft* (very brisk). This measure is a transition from one tempo to another, and as such it requires special attention from the conductor:

As usual, the conductor must first imagine how the music should go, without any regard for arm motions. Only then can one look for the technical means to achieve it. The question is, At what speed should the last eighth note go, and how should the new tempo be shown?

First of all, the note has no fermata. This seems to indicate that it should be played at about the normal eighth note speed in the measure, most likely with some ritard. A ritard is not explicitly asked for, but it might be expected at the end of this rubato introduction. And the fermata before the last eighth acts as a written-out ritard, after which playing in tempo might seem out of place.

The *sehr lebhaft* should come as a surprise and not be prepared by having the eighth drawn out too much. One can get a feeling for its length by conducting the last half of the measure in eighths, without a fermata but with a ritard. Keep this length in mind after adding the fermata, and do not allow the technical problem of showing the new tempo to change that length. Most likely Hindemith did not have a specific relationship in mind between the two tempos, and one should avoid forcing such a relationship. While it is true that related tempos are easier to work with, that is not a sufficient reason for adopting them.

After conducting the triplets—quite possibly by beating all of them—the conductor reaches the fermata on the third beat. At this point the conductor's beat should continue slowly toward the fourth beat, go beyond it (which is the normal case), and then give four as a subdivided beat. The motion for the last eighth note should start as if there were no tempo change in the next measure. Then, as the conductor feels when the eighth will be over, the remainder of the upbeat must be in the new tempo. Had the piece begun at the *sehr lebhaft* at mm 176, one would have given two preparatory beats, but in this situation we can be assured that the players will be paying a great deal of attention to the upbeat.

The technique of giving a beat with its proper curve, but at a certain point changing the speed to show the new tempo, is an excellent way of making many transitions work naturally. The difficulty is in having the right amount of time in the first measure while giving an unrelated upbeat for the next:

Typical upbeat, at a m.m. speed of 60 (1 second)
Time line goes from right to left to coincide with direction of arm motion

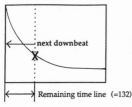

next downbeat

Time line = m.m. 60
X = new upbeat at m.m. 132 (time remaining before next downbeat)

Remaining time line   (=132)

In this example the time line, which proceeds from the upbeat to the next measure, is shown traveling from right to left because that is the direction in which the arm gives the upbeat. This imaginary line is shown in the previous example. The dotted vertical line that intersects the conducting motion shows where the new upbeat is to start, and that upbeat must not change the overall length of the time line. It is also possible for the conductor's beat to stop and wait for the time line to approach the next bar before becoming the new upbeat, but only if the last beat has no rhythmic activity on it.

In the next example, fermatas occur on every conceivable rhythmic point in the measures, which are also in a great variety of meters. In addition, they are often followed by tempo changes. This example encompasses measures 18 to 28 of the fourth movement of Boulez's *Le Marteau sans Maître*. Written in 1954, it is considered one of the most difficult works of the twentieth century:

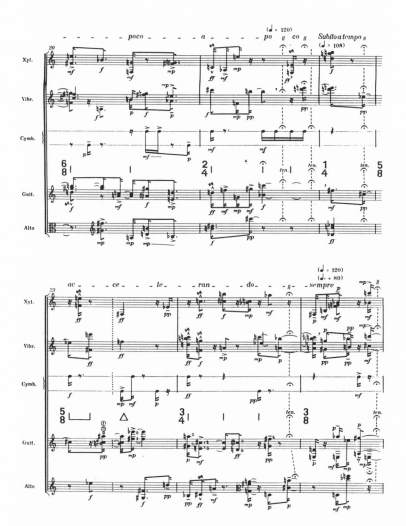

The reason for placing some of the fermatas between notes (not actually on a note or a rest) has to do with which notes ring through the fermata and which are short and do not last into the fermata. In measure 28 the fermata occurs after the first eighth, and the tempo is quarter = 120. After giving the downbeat, which is immediately followed by a fermata, there is no way to bring in the instruments again without giving another quarter beat of preparation—another downbeat. This work requires that the conductor break the rule of one downbeat per measure many times. The upbeat, too, presents a problem. Just in these eleven measures, the upbeat unit will be either an eighth, a quarter, a dotted quarter, or two eighths. They are marked in the example, and of course they pertain to what type of rhythm follows them. Needing differing upbeats is not something new, but the profusion of them in this work is unusual.

Another difficulty of this work is that the tempos are so fast. The normal fast tempo is quarter = 208.[1] Here are two typical pages from the first movement:

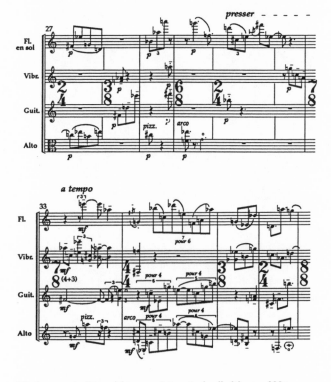

---

[1] In the second edition of this score, interestingly, all of the mm 208 tempos were changed to mm 168.

We also find an example, at the beginning of the third movement, of a measure containing four triplet quarters:

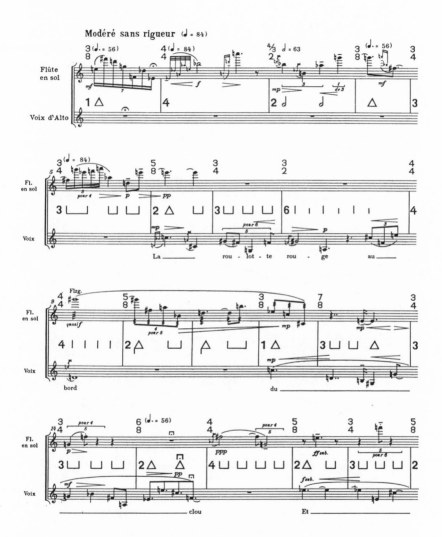

The tempo indication of half note = 78 suggests that it should be conducted in two. We can see from these measures that the conductor needs to have command over the tempo shifts, which are like metric modulations, but without any continuing metric units.

Conducting Metric Modulations

There are two basic types of metric modulation. In one, the inner units that are part of the modulation appear on both sides of the dividing line. At the point of the modulation they become part of a new grouping, and because the new grouping is either larger or smaller than the previous one, the beat, and thus the tempo, becomes either slower or faster. To accomplish this, it is essential that the conductor be completely comfortable with hearing fast inner units and then be able to group them into any size called for by the music. The most difficult groupings will involve fives and sevens. Here are some examples from Elliott Carter's Double Concerto (meas. 30–35):

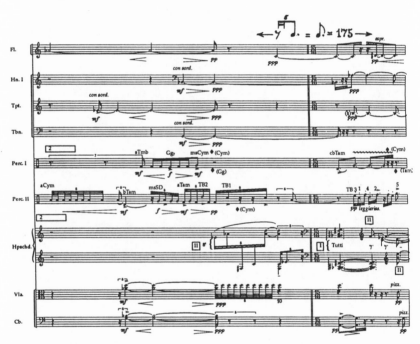

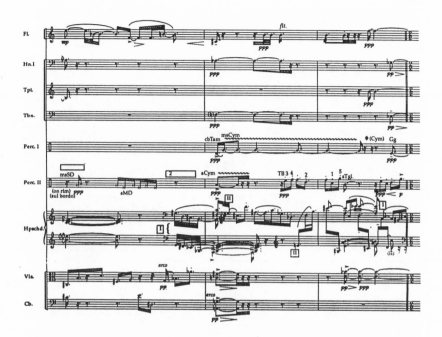

DOUBLE CONCERTO FOR HARPSICHORD, PIANO AND TWO CHAMBER ORCHESTRAS, by Elliot Carter. Copyright © 1964 Associated Music Publishers, Inc. International Copyright Secured. All Rights Reserved. Used by Permission.

It is not unusual in works involving metric modulation for the tempo indications to contain fractions, such as 52.5. In fact, much of this section of the Double Concerto is subdivided into quarters which equal mm 105 (2 × 52.5).

The first modulation uses a unit, a dotted eighth quintuplet, that exists only fleetingly as the last note played by the harpsichord just before the 15/16 measure. This cannot be worked with directly, especially since there is a gap of one quintuplet sixteenth before going on. Instead, the speed of quintuplet sixteenths is used as the speed for the next normal sixteenths. (Since we are told that a dotted eighth quintuplet equals a dotted eighth, we know that a quintuplet sixteenth must equal a sixteenth). Therefore, this modulation requires the conductor to group quintuplet sixteenths into threes, then regroup the threes into fives at measure 35 to go back to normal quarters. Incidentally, although the meter at this point is listed as 2/2, the proper meter to conduct is 4/4—that is, a four pattern rather than 2/2 subdivided. The only reason to conduct in a subdivided 2/2 pattern would be if the music had rhythms of more than a half note, or if that unit had to be used for another modulation. A bit later in this section we do have that situation:

The quarter, however, should still be used because of the intricate rhythms in the other parts, and because the sevens can more easily stay on track when the subdivisions are seen. This would be a good place for either the two-hand approach or the type of subdividing that only shows a very small subdivision.

Carter is one of the small number of composers who feel that seven sixteenths is in the space of eight sixteenths instead of four sixteenths:

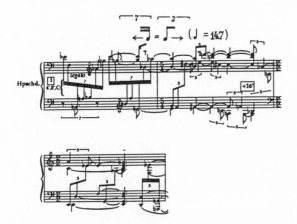

This example is similar to the last, except that sevens are being used instead of fives. The conductor must hear the septuplets and then turn them into triplets. Theoretically the harpsichordist has no problem in keeping all the inner units at the same speed, but the other players depend on the conductor for the placement of their notes. The 5/4 measure uses the pattern of five independent beats, followed by a 4/4 rather than a 2/2 pattern.

The next example is at an even faster tempo:

The normal sixteenths turn into septuplet thirty-seconds. (Here is an example of why many composers would rather use sixteenths for the septuplets instead of thirty-seconds: they continue across the modulation without changing speed, but their look has certainly changed, making it harder to recognize what is happening.)

This example is at such a high speed that it is not possible to actually count the septuplets. They must simply be felt.

Although the Double Concerto is full of illuminating examples, I shall only mention one more involving normal metric modulations, and then go on to describe a special type involving both accelerandos and ritards:

The 6/8 before the second modulation has fours, fives, and sevens over the two main beats. The flutist is told that the quintuplet lasts for a dotted quarter in the 3/4 measure, but the rhythm cannot be played that way unless the flutist could continue to see a dotted quarter. The only way this can happen is if the conductor conducts 2×3, but it is not worth doing this for one player only playing one beat.

The bass, at the modulation, has a rhythm written in normal 3/4 meter. Obviously it is a continuation of the string of dotted eighths from before the modulation. However, if the bassist tries to play it as a new rhythm in 3/4, the likelihood is that it will be different from the previous dotted eighths. The way all these problems are reconciled is for the conductor to ignore all the rhythms in measure 57 except the cellos', because those eighths are the units that will give the tempo for the 3/4 measure, eighth = eighth. The flute and the bass will ignore the conductor and finish their rhythms in the same way they were played in the previous measure.

Ignoring the conductor must be done with careful consideration, and only after making sure that the passage will be played correctly. In this case they are not particularly hard rhythms. Here is another example where the best solution is for one of the players to ignore the conductor:

In the last measure before the modulation, the percussionist has the simplest rhythm imaginable. The quarters become dotted eighths, which correspond to 4×3 in the 3/4 measure, a rhythm made much more difficult because there is no preparation for it. Carter obviously wanted those notes to continue at the same speed, mm 140. The conductor must change speeds precisely, and the percussionist must read the change immediately and play the dotted eighths correctly. This is unlikely to work perfectly, but it is easy for the percussionist to ignore the conductor and go on with the quarter beats. The conductor can then get the new tempo from listening to the percussionist and producing three beats against the players' four.

A similar example comes from Ives's *Three Places in New England:*

THREE PLACES IN NEW ENGLAND, by Charles Ives. Copyright © 1935 and 1976, Mercury Music Corporation. Used by Permission of the Publisher, Theodore Presser Company.

Here Ives juxtaposed two marches at different tempos. They are related in the same way as in the last example—4×3, with four beats of the faster march fitting in three beats of the slower one. One might imagine that conducting 4×3 would solve the problem. But this will not work because there are no three-beat measures, and to have one hand beating a three pattern and the other a four pattern is far too difficult to be practical. Luckily, Ives has already shown us the rewritten version, which is completely adequate for all of the players in the fast march except the trumpet. The others have only to deal with conventional rhythms that fit into the slower meter. In fact, the trumpet can also be rewritten, but the result would be so awkward and obscure that the player would find it almost impossible to play what is really a simple and familiar melody (and if the player did not know the melody, the rewritten rhythm would hardly suggest it). Again, the solution is for the trumpet to ignore the conductor, literally by not watching, and listen to the simple, steady beat produced by the faster group. The original melody is then played in four, with no problems.

Carter has developed a special type of metric modulation that is used in conjunction with a series of ritards or accelerandos:

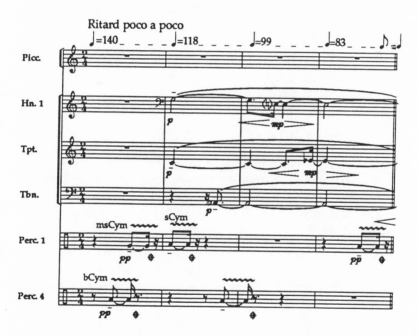

(continued on next page)

(*continued from p. 129*)

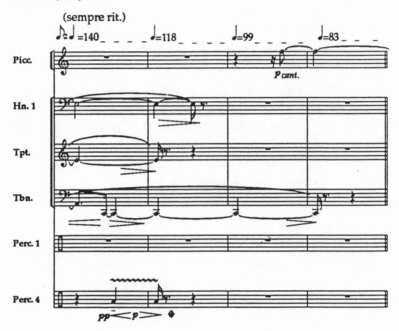

Each group of four measures slows to exactly half the starting speed, at which point it modulates back to the original speed, and so on. Most conductors would have trouble making such precise ritards. They call for looking ahead and noticing where one is at all times, otherwise one or both of the tempos at the modulation will be wrong. This would be apparent to the players and the audience, who are supposed to hear one continuous ritard. The players of the ritarding line have a simpler task than the conductor, because once they are led up to the point of the modulation they will continue with the same speed of note (not counting the minute ritard between any two notes). It is up to the conductor to arrive at the correct speed that allows the doubling of note values to continue the steady ritard. When the last beat before the modulation is reached, the conductor can subdivide by stopping the beat and then going on at twice the tempo. This will alert the players to the modulation, but the conductor must be careful also to follow the player who goes on with no apparent change in tempo.

The same situation occurs with an accelerando, except that in this example it covers eight measures and triples in speed, making it quite a bit more difficult:

Carter helps by showing the approximate speeds at each measure. Incidentally, this is a good technique to use on all accelerandos or ritards that cover a fair amount of time and arrive at a specific tempo. In the present example, the beat starts with quarters and in the last measure or two goes into one (a dotted half), which at the modulation again becomes a quarter. The conducting pattern starts out being fairly wide and gradually narrows as the tempo precludes such large motions, then goes into a beat in one by means of a different type of pattern. This is shown in a comparison of sizes at the start, in the middle, and in the last two measures:

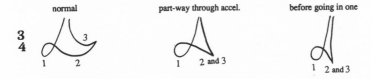

Carter's reason for resorting to this elaborate scheme is to allow an accelerando to be heard at the same time as a long melodic line that does not have an accelerando.

The special pattern for three, which involves showing the first beat and then combining the last two beats, has many uses in music with rapidly changing meter. In 5/8, for example, it has the advantage of showing a quarter instead of a dotted quarter, thus providing a faster beat for greater accuracy.

Analyzing a Score for Conducting

The twentieth century has seen a number of different compositional styles. Some differ only slightly from one another, while others are entirely unique. Many composers have taken elements from several styles, and there is a continuing style that follows the mainstream and is only developmentally different from the past. That difference is mostly in the area of rhythm—the introduction of metric modulation and the use of fives and sevens.

On opening a score written in the last half of the twentieth century, the conductor is likely to find many unfamiliar things, starting with the list of percussion instruments. This family of instruments has undergone a revolutionary expansion. A conductor should know something about most of them, even though they will often be listed in another language and many cannot be found in the dictionary. Using the wrong instrument can hurt the music. Even percussionists have a hard time figuring out which instruments are being called for, and some of the rarer ones cannot even be found in the United States. For example, several European composers have written for tuned plate gongs, as many as twelve at a time. These are unavailable in America and have to be improvised by various means, such as a combination of tuned nipple gongs in conjunction with other "incorrect" instruments. Obviously, the sound is not the same.

Also at the beginning of the score the conductor may find a list of symbols that occur in the work. The number of symbols can range from two or three to forty or fifty. In works involving electronic music or electronically amplified instruments, the composer may need to explain the precise equipment called for and how it is to be used. The same is true of live music mixed with taped elements that needs to be coordinated in one of several ways. In the 1950s and 1960s, a number of composers used such electronic devices as ring modulators that altered the sounds. All these devices and techniques require explanation.

The next thing to determine is whether the score is in C. When we say that a score is in C, we mean that the instruments sound as written (*klingt wie notiert*), with the usual octave transpositions for contrabass, piccolo, and several of the high-pitched members of the bell family. Why shouldn't it be obvious whether the score is in C? With the advent in the early twentieth century of atonal music and twelve-tone music, traditional harmony can no longer tell us which note should be played. That information can only be gleaned after an often exhausting compositional analysis of the work, something that most conductors would not have the time or inclination to do. If one has access to the parts, a quick look at the parts for the transposing instruments will give the answer. If the score is in C, the lowest written notes for the English horn (which is tuned in F) and the alto flute (in G) are:

low ranges for Alto flute and English Horn:

Rarely are these instruments used without exploiting their low registers, since apart from color it is the low notes which distinguish them from the other members of their families.If notes lower than these appear, then we know that the score is not in C.

Many works do not use either of these instruments, so that other ways of telling whether the score is in C must be found. The other transposing instruments are the clarinet, French horn, and trumpet. The lowest notes on the clarinet vary by a half step, depending on the make of instrument, and the very lowest note might not be used, so this is not a reliable source. Neither is the trumpet, since the upper and lower ranges are not absolute but depend on the capabilities of the particular player. Like the trumpet, the French horn has a variable low range; its upper limit, however, is quite uniform, at least within a step or so for all players. Since the horn's normal transposition is a fifth lower than written, anything above the normal upper limit means that the score is not in C:

upper French Horn range:

This method will not work if the upper range is not used. But rather than relying on such detective work by the conductor, composers should avoid any confusion by clearly stating whether or not the score is in C.

Almost all conductors mark their scores, both as an aid in learning the work and as a reminder of what to do at a particular moment. The markings have to do with rhythm, instrument identification, and wanting to make changes in certain aspects of the score. We also have to contend with the so-called short score, which some publishers produce to save money. The short score leaves out any instrument that is not playing, so that the physical layout of each page is not consistent: on one page, say, the clarinet part may be directly above the trombone part, but on the next page the bassoon and trumpet parts may intervene. Some scores have blank space when an instrument is not playing; that is, the staff is left out entirely. This makes it hard to keep track of which instrument is playing. Another thing that publishers do in the interests of saving money is to publish a "composer's facsimile." Although some composers have impeccable handwriting and take care that the notes and measures line up properly, all too many of them produce scores so muddled that many conductors will not even bother to look at them. The result can be grave misunderstandings and much wasted rehearsal time.

Metric and Rhythmic Symbols

As we have seen, the irregular meters, such as 9/8, 10/8, and 11/8, are made up of combinations of twos and threes. Sometimes the ordering of twos and threes is apparent, but often it is not, and the conductor and players need to agree on what it will be in each measure. Composers often forget that measures of rest in irregular meters are more confusing to count than measures with notes. In a typical sequence of rests those players who are counting may have no idea of the particular patterns. Since they count in twos and threes, particularly for sevens and larger, they look to the conductor's beat for confirmation. The ideal situation would be where every measure of rest had within it rests fitting the pattern:

$$\frac{5}{8} \, \text{♪}\,\text{♪·} \mid \text{♪·}\,\text{♪} \mid \frac{7}{8} \, \text{♪·}\,\text{♪♪} \mid \text{♪♪}\,\text{♪·} \mid \text{etc. or:} \; \frac{5}{8} \, \sqcup \triangle \mid \triangle \sqcup \mid$$

This is impractical, though, for long rests, partly because in fast tempos it is much more confusing to look from measure to measure of rests than it is to play notes. In some pieces, a series of 5/8 or 7/8 measures will always have the same layout of fives and sevens. Once the conductor points this out to the players, they can count more easily.

There are a number of symbols for groupings of twos and threes. Conductors must choose the one they think is best. The earliest attempt was probably by Stravinsky, who used dotted lines within the measure:

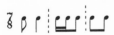

This works fairly well for the individual players, although there is a chance of their mistaking the dotted lines for bar lines. But it can cause problems for the conductor, who needs to have a picture of the whole measure before starting it.

If we look at the individual parts, we are likely to see a series of strokes placed over each of the groupings:

This goes back to earlier music where the question was, Is 3/4 in one or three, is 4/4 in four or two, is 2/2 in two or four? Sometimes the players would write in the word *two* or *four*. For a conductor, the strokes are easy to see and can be useful in a number of situations, but they do not give any information about what is within the main beats.

Another system uses note values:

But this leads to confusion over rests:

Later in the century this problem was overcome by beaming notes and rests so that the result showed the groupings:

Still another system has numbers representing the subdivisions:

The most recent development uses the following symbols:

They stand for two eighths on the first beat and three eighths on the second, and usually mean there are no further subdivisions. The symbol for two is often inverted:

But this is not as good because it is also the symbol for a down-bow.

I have proposed a further refinement of these symbols to help distinguish the units of the beat:

The regular symbols, applied to all the measures, would not visually distinguish between sixteenths, eighths, and quarters:

⊔ = ♩ or ♪

This might result in some players playing at the wrong speed of note. The following symbols would avert this problem:

This system could be extended to thirty-seconds:

etc.

Occasionally, in some of the larger irregular meters, the groupings might include a quarter. In 9/8, for example, we might see $2+3+4$, and this calls for another symbol:

$\frac{9}{8}$ ⊔ △ □ |

In addition to these symbols, which delineate what goes on within the measure, there is need for a symbol to show the number of beats in the pattern for the overall measure. This pertains to time signatures that are larger than 7/8 or 7/4:

$\frac{11}{8}$ ⊔ ⊔ ⊔ △ ⊔ | $\frac{10}{8}$ ⊔ △ △ ⊔ | ⊔ ⊔ ⊔ ⊔ ⊔ |

These large measures can contain three, four, even five or more beats. This information must be available at the start of the measure. It could be shown by printing the number of beats with a circle around it to indicate that those beats will be a combination of twos and threes:

⑤   ④   ⑤
$\frac{11}{8}$ |$\frac{10}{8}$ |$\frac{10}{8}$ |

The words *ritard* and *accelerando* have always been used instead of symbols. This has served quite well until around the middle of the twentieth century, when a number of composers began to use these familiar devices in highly structured ways, such as to connect unrelated tempos. Ritards and accelerandos can cover one beat or many measures. They can delineate a large tempo change or a small one. A simple symbol can convey much of this information:

A rising arrow means *accelerando;* a falling arrow means *ritard.* The steeper the slope, the sharper the change of speed. If the change is over many measures, approximations of the tempo can be put at various places on the arrow. The arrow can also point to the exact spot where the change is leading.

Many pieces have been written that continually change tempo. Here is an early example, from Schoenberg's *Erwartung* (1909):

Many of the tempos are not mathematically related, and the conductor can arrive at a new tempo and not remember what the old one was. Of course, one should know the music well enough to avoid this problem, and Schoenberg's music is certainly the type that allows one to learn the tempos. But they do change often, and sometimes only incrementally, so that the conductor may not know even whether to go slower or faster. This problem is more pronounced in recent music, because of the fact that it may not be based on familiar principles. A simple solution is to place the old metronome speed in parenthesis just before the new one:

Players also have the problem of knowing if the new tempo is slower or faster, and they are unlikely to know the music as well as the conductor does. It can be a big help to them to put an arrow up or down just before the change:

Index